ANGEL DOGS

Allen and Linda Anderson are authors and inspirational speakers. They co-founded the Angel Animals Network, dedicated to increasing love and respect for all life through the power of story.

In addition to *Angel Dogs: When Best Friends Become Heroes*, their books together are *Angel Animals: Exploring Our Spiritual Connection with Animals*, *God's Messengers: What Animals Teach Us About the Divine*, *Angel Cats: Divine Messengers of Comfort* and *Rainbows & Bridges: An Animal Companion Memorial Kit*. Their next book in this series will be *Angel Horses: Divine Messengers of Hope*.

In 2004 Allen and Linda Anderson were recipients of a Certificate of Commendation from Governor Tim Pawlenty in recognition of their contributions as authors enhancing the economy and welfare of the State of Minnesota.

Allen Anderson is a computer software specialist, writer and photographer. He was profiled in Jackie Waldman's book *The Courage to Give*. Linda Anderson is an award-winning playwright as well as a screenwriter and fiction writer. She is the author of *35 Golden Keys to Who You Are & Why You're Here*. Allen and Linda teach writing at The Loft Literary Center in Minneapolis, where Linda was awarded The Anderson Residency for Outstanding Loft Teachers. The Andersons share their home with a dog, two cats and a cockatiel. They donate a portion of revenue from their projects to animal shelters and animal welfare organizations.

You are welcome to visit Allen and Linda Anderson's website (www.angelanimals.net) and to send them stories and letters about your spiritual experiences with animals for possible future publication. At the website or by email you may also request a subscription to the free online publication *Angel Animals Story of the Week*, through which you'll receive a new inspiring story each week.

Contact Allen and Linda Anderson at:

Angel Animals Network

P.O. Box 26354

Minneapolis, MN 55426

Website: www.angelanimals.net

Email: angelanimals@angelanimals.net

ANGEL dogs

When best friends become heroes

Allen & Linda Anderson

PENGUIN BOOKS

PENGUIN BOOKS

Published by the Penguin Group
Penguin Books Ltd, 80 Strand, London WC2R ORL, England
Penguin Group (USA), Inc., 375 Hudson Street, New York, New York 10014, USA
Penguin Group (Canada), 90 Eglinton Avenue East, Suite 700, Toronto, Ontario, Canada M4P 2Y3
(a division of Pearson Penguin Canada Inc.)
Penguin Ireland, 25 St Stephen's Green, Dublin 2, Ireland (a division of Penguin Books Ltd)
Penguin Group (Australia), 250 Camberwell Road, Camberwell, Victoria 3124, Australia
(a division of Pearson Australia Group Pty Ltd)
Penguin Books India Pvt Ltd, 11 Community Centre, Panchsheel Park, New Delhi – 110 017, India
Penguin Group (NZ), 67 Apollo Drive, Rosedale, North Shore 0632, New Zealand
(a division of Pearson New Zealand Ltd)
Penguin Books (South Africa) (Pty) Ltd, 24 Sturdee Avenue, Rosebank, Johannesburg 2196, South Africa

Penguin Books Ltd, Registered Offices: 80 Strand, London WC2R ORL, England

www.penguin.com

First published in the United States of America by New World Library 2005
First published in Great Britain in Penguin Books 2009
1

Printed in Great Britain by Clays Ltd, St Ives plc

A CIP catalogue record for this book is available from the British Library

ISBN: 978–0–141–39984–3

www.greenpenguin.co.uk

Contents

Chapter One
Have You Received Loyalty and Friendship from Divine Messenger Dogs?

Chapter Two
What If Heroes Have Four Paws and Fur?

Chapter Three
Can You Catch Joyrides on Wagging Tails?   91

Chapter Four
Are Dogs Your Divine Prescription for Better Health?   129

Chapter Five
Have Dogs Discovered the Doorways to Heaven? 167

Foreword

by Willard Scott

I love all animals, but I have a special place in my heart for dogs. We always had dogs — some years, lots of them, as many as five dogs at a time. They would just "show up," and we could never find who they belonged to. They didn't have identification. After no one claimed them, we kept the dogs. No dog was turned away. We lived out in the country, and sometimes I wonder if the word just got around: "Show up at that house on the hill and you'll have a great life!" And they did. They were well fed and well loved.

Our dogs were a big part of our family life. They gave us the gifts of love, protection, and comfort in the sad and tough times, and with their barking, they even kept the crows out of the garden. Dogs really are our very best friends.

Reading *Angel Dogs: Divine Messengers of Love* is like taking a walk in the park on a sunny day with your favorite dog. This wonderful collection of stories will bring back memories of the sweet, delightful, and touching times you have spent with your own loyal canine friends.

Starting with a bit about the history of the human-dog relationship, *Angel Dogs* then presents stories that run the gamut of people's relationships with dogs. The real-life experiences in this book show remarkable dogs serving as heroes, healers, playful friends, and spiritual partners. These dogs work side by side with people whose lives are made happier and healthier by their presence.

Dogs have their own unique, loving ways to let us know that in times of crisis, in times of celebration, in times of daily life, we are not alone. A wag of the tail, a lick, and a hug, are some of the not too subtle ways that dogs express their love. Each day, a dog tells you, "I adore you!"

As diverse as each of us are, a love for dogs brings people together. Just try walking down your neighborhood street with a cute puppy and see the smiles on the faces of the people passing you. Often a crowd will gather, as neighbors stop to admire and appreciate the newest addition to your family. It's easy to understand why. Dogs offer one of the most stable and enduring friendships on this earth.

I love *Angel Dogs*. Its stories and messages will amaze and delight you. Allen and Linda Anderson's book will make a wonderful gift for all your dog-loving friends, for anyone who is considering adopting or rescuing a dog, and for those who have lost a beloved dog.

Read it and marvel at what the world looks like through the eyes of some of God's most loving creatures.

ANGEL
dogs

Spiritual Guide Dogs

At the time I needed to learn a lot — about connection and close-ness and safety — and something deep inside whispered, A dog, you need a dog, and I was lucky enough, or open enough, to listen.

— Caroline Knapp,
Pack of Two: The Intricate Bond between People and Dogs

Four paws pad lightly on the ground next to two feet as a dog and human companion go for a walk. No relationship between people and animals is as complex as that represented by the simple act of a human being out for a stroll with a dog.

The person gazes at a cloudless blue sky lit by a searing sun, at a variety of houses along the way, at a neighbor ambling by who makes eye contact. The dog-walking person pieces together what the human brain takes in and uses language to compose fleeting thoughts into a story: *Looks like it's going to be a scorcher today. Hope I'm wearing enough sunscreen. My neighbor better water his lawn. Wonder if I look as out of shape as she does.*

The dog, with two hundred million scent receptors to the human's five million, sniffs the ground, inspects fallen leaves and broken twigs, picks up scents from other dogs and the soles of human shoes, and occasionally smells the approach of another dog. Every odor passes through scent membranes and is cataloged by a brain in which each smell tells a story. The dog's brain whirs with the assault of heightened olfactory, visual, and auditory impressions. Without benefit of human language, of course, the dog thinks: *This is a dog I've never met before. That woman carries treats in her pocket and gives me one if my human stops to talk with her. This is where I last peed. We usually cross the street on that corner. A siren is coming.*

Diverse as their worldviews might be, humans and dogs have one of the most stable and enduring friendships on earth. Stanley Coren, in *How Dogs Think* writes, "Even more striking is data from a recent scientific study from the dog-genome project. Ewen Kirkness of the Institute for Genomic Research in Rockville, Maryland, and his research team compared the DNA of a poodle to that of a human. What they found was that there was more than a 75 percent overlap between the genetic codes of humans and canines."[1]

So although the two species have much in common, they also complement each other by doing, viewing, and experiencing life in vastly different ways. They make up for each other's abilities or inabilities to cope with and thrive on this planet. No wonder dogs and humans had to find each other. Once they did, the two species became inseparable.

How Humans Got Together with Their Best Friends

Studies published in the journal *Science* by the biologist Jennifer Leonard, from the Smithsonian's National Museum of Natural History, in Washington, D.C., analyzed mitochondrial DNA (mtDNA), passed on only in a matriarchal line. Leonard found, "The transition from wolf to dog took place exclusively on the Eurasian landmass. When the first humans crossed to North America from eastern Asia, they brought their newly domesticated canines with them."[2] Peter Savolainen, of Stockholm's Royal Institute of Technology, looked at how much mtDNA varied within dog populations and compared dog and wolf mtDNA. Savolainen estimates that the genetic branching of wolves into dogs "began 15,000 years ago, if three families of wolves were involved, or 40,000, if the entire process began with a single family."[3]

As authors of this book of inspiring true stories, we're not claiming to be dog historians. But we found a wonderful website, AustralianMedia.com, which has a page, "History of Dogs," that pulls together a wealth of information showing how attitudes toward dogs through the ages moved from utilitarian to adulatory. Here are some interesting facts from the website.

During the Stone Age, tamed dogs helped humans to hunt. Ancient Egyptians made pets of a dog they called saluki, from an Arabic word meaning "noble one." Greyhounds, dalmatians, and mastiffs are thought to be among the oldest dog breeds; they were used in hunting and war. Greek mythology honors Cerberus, a three-headed dog who guards the entrance to Hades. The Mayans thought that Nahua Xolotl, or Pek, the dog of lightning, announced the arrival of death.

In the Middle Ages, dogs were status symbols. The number of dogs and variety of breeds a person had were measurements of prosperity. Kings, nobles, and church officials developed purebreds for hunting and sport.

Hebrew and Muslim cultures used dogs to help shepherds with their flocks, but they considered canines to be unclean. At the other end of the spectrum, during the Roman Empire, people started keeping dogs as beloved pets, and dogs were honored in sculptures and portraits as members of the family.

In the royal courts of the Far East, dogs were so esteemed that they had their own human servants, who waited on them and catered to their canine needs. The Tibetan terrier could not be bought or sold but was considered valuable because of the belief that this breed was a luck bringer.

In Victorian-era Europe, the lapdog became popular as a companion to the ladies of the court, and Great Danes and mastiffs were outfitted with spiked collars and suits of armor to accompany soldiers into battle. Meanwhile, in America, dogs accompanied parishioners to church services and served as foot warmers while the humans prayed and listened to lengthy sermons.[4]

According to Brad Zellar, in his review of *A Dog's History of America*, by Mark Derr: "Dogs, in fact, have served, and continue to serve, in every capacity imaginable; they have been guards, scouts, hunters, herders, gladiators, and beasts of burden. They have gone to war, to space, and to the ends of the earth; starred in films, been recognized as heroes, died on vivisection tables, and provided succor to presidents and poor wretches (and presidents who were poor wretches) down through the centuries. To this day, dogs are an increasingly visible presence in law enforcement, airport security details, hospitals, and popular culture."[5]

Perhaps one of the most fascinating and closest associations has been between Native Americans and dogs. PetPlace Veterinarians' website, on the page titled "The History of Dogs and Native Americans," explains the place of reverence that dogs held in Native American culture. The website says that Native Americans believe dogs *chose* to become the companions of humans. About twelve thousand years ago, the wolf populations began to spend more time with people. Some wolves were probably more playful and social than others. The wolf pack, a structured group disinclined to put up with antics among its members, rejected brethren with friendlier personalities. These friendly wolves gravitated toward Native American camps, looking for leaders and a hierarchical pack. The Native Americans welcomed the sweet-natured dogs, relied on them as useful hunters and protectors, and viewed them as family members, giving them names. "When Native Americans left their homes to hunt, they departed knowing that the dogs would protect their wives, mothers, children, and even livestock. If someone was lost, the dog's keen sense of smell was used to search [for] and find the missing person. The dog's bravery, courage, and loyalty sealed a place in the annals of American tribal life.... Tribes revered dogs and included them in religious ceremonies, believing dogs helped people navigate the journey to the afterlife."[6]

One of the most fascinating accounts in Native American folklore is the legend of the Ojibwe, or Chippewa, a tribe of Algonquian-speaking North American Indians of the Upper Great Lakes. Samoyed.org's website shares this story passed down through the generations, which we retell below.

According to the legend, two hungry and lost Ojibwe drifted in their canoe onto a strange shore. When they landed on the beach, they saw the footprints of a giant. Soon, the biggest man they'd ever seen came walking toward them. They were frightened, but the giant turned out to be kind and invited the Ojibwe to go home with him. The two Ojibwe were hungrier than they were frightened, so they gratefully accepted the giant's invitation.

Later that night, a Windigo, an evil spirit, came into the giant's lodge. The Windigo didn't look evil at first. But after visiting for a while, the Windigo took the giant aside and said, "I want those two Ojibwe. I'm going to eat them."

When the giant refused to turn over the Ojibwe, the Windigo flew into a rage. He accidentally overturned a big bowl on the floor of the giant's lodge. Underneath the bowl was an animal who looked something like a wolf. The giant told the Windigo, "This one is Dog." Then he told Dog to kill the Windigo.

Upon hearing the giant's command, Dog grew huge and fierce. He jumped on the Windigo and killed him. The Ojibwe couldn't believe their eyes. When the giant saw how impressed they were, he told Dog to go home with the two men as his gift to them.

At the shore the next morning, Dog grew as big as a horse. The Ojibwe men got on top of his back. The giant waved good-bye. Dog plunged into the water and started swimming, with the Ojibwe still riding him.

Before the lost Ojibwe arrived at a familiar shore, Dog grew small again. So the Ojibwe swam the rest of the way home, with Dog paddling after them. He followed them to their lodges. Then he vanished into the forest.

The Ojibwe tribe was happy to see their lost brothers again. But no one would believe the story about the strange animal named Dog.

A few days later, Dog came trotting out of the forest. The men he'd rescued returned the favor by feeding him wonderful meals. So Dog decided to stay from that day on. And of course, everyone was happy to know such a brave and generous creature would now be part of their tribal family. This is how Dog came to earth.[7]

In modern times, it is as if legends and myths about the origins of dogs and their relationships with humans have grown and multiplied. Dogs help children learn how to read through the Paws to Read program in Pleasanton, California. Service dogs aid the visually and hearing impaired and the physically and mentally disabled. Search-and-rescue dogs, medic-alert dogs, and cancer-sniffing dogs, who can detect cancer in humans and in lab specimens with cancer cells in them, save lives every day. It's no wonder that millions have concluded that Dog really did come to earth as a gift from some otherworldly home.

The Emotional and Spiritual Lives of Dogs

We have lived with dogs for most of our lives. It has also been our privilege to collect thousands of true anecdotes from people who write about the positive effect that dogs have had on their lives. Over the years, we have been able to publish their stories in our series of books and newsletters, and on our Angel Animals Network website. After reviewing the accounts people have sent to us about their experiences with dogs, we have concluded that there are two under-reported aspects in which the lives of dogs and humans intersect with amazing similarity and regularity: *emotional* and *spiritual*.

Dogs act as honest-to-a-fault barometers of human emotion. Brother Christopher, from the Monks of New Skete Monastery, in Cambridge, New York, is an author who raises and breeds German shepherds. He says, "Interestingly enough, a relationship with a dog also helps us know ourselves better. A dog is guileless and utterly honest. It becomes a unique mirror reflecting us back to ourselves, if we pay attention."[8]

Much has been written about the emotions of dogs. Even the most rigid scientific studies have had to admit that dogs experience the emotion of fear. But people who actually live with dogs, rather than studying them in artificial settings, know that dogs exhibit a full range of emotions: joy, sadness, anger, amusement, optimism, anticipation, attachment, and satisfaction, among others. Joseph Wood Krutch writes about the intensity of emotion that animals feel: "It is difficult to see how one can deny that the dog, apparently beside himself at the prospect of a walk... is experiencing a joy the intensity of which it is beyond our power to imagine much less to share. In the same way his dejection can at least appear to be no less bottomless."[9]

What is less frequently discussed, probably because of pressure from skeptics who worry about mawkish sentimentality and the "sin" of anthropomorphism, is the spiritual nature of dogs. Also, certain religious dogmas don't allow for animals to have souls or a spiritual nature. Yet the stories you are about to read have been written by many people who may have started out with doubts but have witnessed for themselves that dogs exhibit spiritual qualities in abundance. Dogs can be wise, compassionate, loyal, courageous, self-sacrificing, and altruistic. Most of all, they can give the purest, most unconditional love.

Many of the storytellers in this book have also experienced dogs as divine messengers. We use the word *angel* when describing dogs, not to say that every dog, at all times, behaves in a traditionally angelic way. The word *angel* harks back to the Greek word *angelos*, which means "messenger." And as you will see, dogs do indeed serve as messengers from Spirit.

Dogs bring to humans such messages as *You are loved. You are not alone. You are protected and guided by a divine higher power.* Dogs deliver messages such as *When you are lonely, weary, overwhelmed by life's burdens, I am here.* People who are in pain often can't hear the voice of God whispering comfort and hope. So God sends them a messenger with a furry face, wagging tail, licking tongue, and generous heart. Those who can accept the gift are taught that love is all around by one of life's wisest teachers.

The mission of this book is to open your heart so you can recognize and receive blessings from Spirit, even if they arrive accompanied by a bark.

The Love Affair with Dogs

Apparently, a lot of people understand that dogs bring special gifts to the lives of those who live with them. According to the American Pet Products Manufacturers Association, its 2003–2004 National Pet Owners Survey revealed that 64.2 million U.S. households have at least one pet. Sixty-five million of these animal family members are dogs. Those with pets spend 31 billion dollars to care for, feed, pamper, and enjoy the animals in their homes.[10] And the need for dog companionship doesn't stop with American pet lovers taking their pooches along for a ride in their car. An article in *USA Weekend*,

"Shopping Hounds: Retailers Go to the Dogs by Inviting Them In," reports a variety of ways that retailers are catering to those in the canine crowd who abhor being separated from their dogs. People in suburban Las Vegas can take their dogs to a store called the District at Green Valley Ranch, where the dogs lounge on the furniture. At a dog-friendly Saks Fifth Avenue in Phoenix's Biltmore Fashion Park,

Teresa and Don Madak's dog Brittany helps Linda sign books

dog biscuits are kept at sales registers, and the store hosts a human-dog tea. Bal Harbour shops, near Miami, provide Dolce & Gabbana water bowls for dogs. Stony Point Fashion Park, an upscale, open-air mall in Richmond, Virginia, has comfort stations for dogs, with plastic bags to collect doggy doo-doo. In the Aspen Grove Lifestyle Center, near Denver, retailers experienced a 13 percent jump in sales when they invited people to shop with their dogs.[11] And of course, New York is heaven on earth for 20 million dogs, with its stores that sell food, supplies, and jewel-encrusted collars just for dogs, and its proliferation of dog parks, dog runs, dog restaurants, dog bakeries, dog nannies, and dog exercise studios. Our own love affair with dogs got a big boost when we met Teresa and Don Madak's dog Brittany at a book event in metro-Atlanta. Brittany sat on Linda's lap and seemed poised to add her own autograph to the books.

Our Angel Dog

We invite you to join our family of canines and humans to celebrate the mystery, the enlightenment, the sheer happiness of the human-dog spiritual connection. Our dog, Taylor, an aging yellow Labrador retriever with boundless energy, a goofy grin, and the sweetness of a Minnesota spring day, has graciously helped us to write and edit this book. She lives mostly peacefully with us and two cats, Cuddles and Speedy, and Sunshine, a talking cockatiel.

Since Taylor often has to negotiate with brothers and sisters who have retractable claws, jumping and flying abilities, and a sharp beak,

Allen and Linda's Taylor as a puppy

we've asked her to share her wisdom about life. She offers an advice column, "Ask Taylor," at the end of each chapter in this book.

About This Book

The contributors to *Angel Dogs* come from various walks of life and different parts of the world. Be sure to read more about them in the Contributors section, which includes their biographies. Many of the stories in this book were winners in the Angel Dogs Contest, which we sponsored prior to finishing this manuscript. Other stories came from people who are among the twenty thousand readers in forty countries of *Angel Animals Story of the Week*, our free online newsletter (www.angelanimals.net) that helps people greet each week with a new and inspiring message from the animal kingdom.

The stories in *Angel Dogs* span the spectrum of the human-animal relationships from this life to the afterlife. They are accounts of incredible dog heroes, gifted dog healers, and loving, loyal dog companions.

As you read the stories and try the meditations that follow them, reflect upon the Angel Dogs who have graced your own life. They are still with you, whether in spirit or in cuddly physical bodies, loving you in ways that only a dog can love.

In the first chapter, you'll meet:

- A marine corporal's dog who won't allow a fallen soldier to be forgotten
- A newly adopted dog who persisted in protecting an infant
- The cell dog who transformed a deaf prisoner into a compassionate and patient man
- A dog who prepared a popular Atlanta radio disc jockey, Jill Kelly, for motherhood
- A mastiff with a massive spiritual message from deep in the heart of the desert
- The dog who chose to cheer seniors as his mission in life
- The dog whose love and friendship became immortalized in a country music song

- And of course Taylor, who shares her wisdom about why dogs are so loyal.

It is our fondest wish that you will read, relax, enjoy, and be inspired by the hopefulness that divine canine messengers bring to this world.

CHAPTER ONE

Have You Received Loyalty and Friendship from Divine Messenger Dogs?

Sometimes animals seem to have been put on the earth for the specific purpose of caring about and helping us. They are powerful forces for good.

— Kristin von Kreisler, *The Compassion of Animals*

After the events of September 11, 2001, Jon Stewart, host and resident satirist on Comedy Central's *The Daily Show*, was devastated, along with most of the world. His way to deal with the tragedy was one that millions have found lifts their spirits as nothing else can: he adopted a puppy.

As America reeled after September 11 from the loss of life and the feeling of vulnerability within its own shores, an unfortunate backlash toward people of Arab descent or Muslim belief occurred in some places. Ahmed Tharwat is the host and producer of *Belahdan*, an Arab American talk show on Public TV, Channel 17 in Minneapolis. A few months after 9/11, Ahmed's daughter persuaded him to adopt a beagle puppy. Later, he wrote a letter to the editor of the *Minneapolis Star Tribune* about taking the puppy for walks and the effects the young dog had on people around them. "Strangers who used to skillfully avoid eye contact now wanted to engage me in warm conversation. Patriotic national hotline tippers, usually more concerned about Muslim sleepers and terrorism, now cordially inquired about my dog's sleeping habits, breed, and big, black eyes. People's interest had taken a blessed turn. Their mood was inviting — families congregated around me to see the cute puppy. For me, a dog single-handedly brought the American melting pot down to a simmer. He accomplished what years of diversity training have failed to do. Regardless of our race or country of origin, we have become a community of dog lovers."[1]

The friendship and loyalty of dogs help human beings to get through just about any of life's changes and sudden curves. This is because dogs are fantastic stress relievers. In a study of 240 couples conducted by Karen Allen, of the State University of New York at Buffalo, when people were tested on stressful tasks in the company of their pets, they coped better than when they were alone or when a friend or spouse was nearby.[2]

Dogs have an enormous capacity for helping people forget their worries and anxieties. The reason is really very simple: dogs are good friends; their loyalty is unswerving. Perhaps this is why 80 percent of the people surveyed in a study by the American Animal Hospital Association selected companionship as their major reason for having a pet.[3]

Dogs have become important to the daily lives and emotional well-being of millions. As a society, we have accepted the obligation to preserve and protect this beneficial relationship. Today, people file lawsuits to uphold the rights of animals. Feuding spouses contest each other in divorce hearings over who will have custody of the dog. It is not at all out of the norm for human companions to spend thousands of dollars for surgeries and other procedures to alleviate the suffering and extend the lives of their ailing and aging pets. Dogs these days are full-fledged members of the family, and as they take over our hearts and homes with their endearing ways, we bestow upon them rights and privileges (as well as clothing and jewelry) that used to belong only to human beings.

Treating dogs as human beings has its up- and downsides. The positive outcome is that the humane treatment of dogs and other animals improves as people become more aware that animals have thoughts, feelings, and even divine purposes. The downside is that at times, it's a burden on the animal when people try to transform a dog into a human. The dogness is obscured or lost. When the lines get too blurred, differences that have made the human-dog relationship complementary and valuable throughout the ages fade away.

The modern inclination is to forget that dogs, as lovable and capable of acting beyond instinct as they are, can and do revert to instinct. The tendency to turn dogs into unquestioning protectors and defenders ignores other aspects of their nature. Just as humans are not all alike, dogs are not all alike. Just as humans behave badly at times, dogs do too.

For example, it could be tempting, especially after you read the stories in this book about dogs saving the lives of infants and toddlers, to think that your dog is an ideal babysitter. But each dog is unique. Some breeds are inclined to herd, and they naturally help to keep children away from danger. Other breeds may have more aggressive natures. And no matter the breed, some dogs may have been subjected to abuse that scarred their emotions and personalities, leaving them anxious, edgy, or overly aggressive. This could mean that in a time of crisis, or if something triggers the dog's instinct to attack, a nearby child (or adult) could be in danger.

One area of concern is when babies are in swings. The back-and-forth swinging motion can send an impulse to the dog to chase prey. Catherine Mills, a North Carolina dog trainer, and John C. Wright, an animal behaviorist with Mercer University, say that "pets should be conditioned to ignore swings before a baby is put into one."[4] As with any relationship, whether with animal or human, it's good to use common sense and always keep an eye on the situation. And of course, be cautious about leaving a baby or young child alone, even with the family pet.

That said, most dogs are astoundingly perceptive, accommodating, and loyal to a fault. They are also masters at forgiveness. In the following stories, notice the number of times dogs have been scheduled for euthanization because of overcrowded animal shelters and irresponsible humans who abandoned them. When the dogs are rescued, they don't hold grudges against humanity, but become people's most enduring friends.

In this chapter you'll meet dogs who went far above and beyond what most humans can or will offer one another in friendship and loyalty. We hope the stories will remind you of the companionship that dogs have brought to your life and the messages of unconditional love that they have imprinted upon your heart.

Cpl. J. R. Dugan Honors a Fallen Soldier

Del Rio, Texas

I named my dog, a Jack Russell terrier who is twenty-three pounds of solid muscle, Cpl. J. R. Dugan, USMC 2164539. I gave him the combination of the initials for his breed, Jack Russell, (J. R.) with my U.S. Marine Corps rank and serial number, because this dog has the heart of a lion. I call him Cpl. J. R. Dugan or Cpl. J. R., for short. He is tricolor with a light brown patch over one eye that makes him look like a little pirate. Cpl. J. R. is fearless and the smartest dog I have ever had. He is the little heartbeat at my feet.

As a Marine Corps infantryman survivor of heavy combat in the Vietnam War, I have always believed that it is important to recognize the courage and bravery of every man or woman who has served in our country's military. What I didn't realize until one late October day in 2003 was that it would be my dog who demonstrated how vital it is that we never forget those who gave their lives so that others could live.

The favorite place for Cpl. J. R. Dugan and me to walk is the Sacred Heart Catholic Cemetery in Del Rio, Texas. This cemetery is one of four cemeteries that are located side by side — Saint Joseph's Catholic Cemetery, Sacred Heart Catholic Cemetery, Westlawn Protestant Cemetery, and the Masonic Cemetery. J. R. and I spend

21

countless hours weaving in and out of all four cemeteries and enjoying the lush trees and abundant wildlife. Numerous species of birds, deer, rabbits, and squirrels populate this oasis in the harsh semi-desert environment of Del Rio. J. R. and I both prefer these pleasant strolls through nature to walking around a circular track.

J. R. and I were having a late-afternoon stroll that started like all the rest of our walks, with the exception of a misting rain and a discernible chill in the air. I had parked my SUV near my family's burial plot and put a light pack on my shoulders. I always carry water, a collapsible water bowl for J. R., J. R.'s first-aid kit, a Swiss Army knife, a snack for both of us, my bird identification field manual, and my trusty Nikon 7x50 binoculars. I made all the pack adjustments, picked up my walking staff, grasped Cpl. J. R.'s leash, and we were off on another adventure.

The wind picked up, and the chill in the air became more pronounced, so I buttoned my windbreaker and pushed my hat a little farther down on my forehead. Cpl. J. R. loved the chill and was prancing like a prize stallion in a parade. I love to watch him be so full of life. Our walks are made more enjoyable by the fact that Cpl. J. R. and I have learned to work as a team. This dog misses nothing. Instead of barking, he always alerts me by making eye contact when he sees something move. After Cpl. J. R. detects animal movement, I can stop and observe the animal with my binoculars.

Our walking trips through the cemeteries are like a time machine that takes us back to the origins of our community. I pass the grave sites of old family friends, mentors, teachers, pioneers, villains, and people who now are known only to God. These are very special walks, since they give me time to reflect and appreciate all the people who helped to make me who I am today.

On this autumn afternoon, Cpl. J. R. and I had walked for nearly an hour when I noticed that he was getting a little tired. He had stopped to show me his extended tongue, his signal that he wanted some water. For our break, I always stop at a little meditation bench in the Masonic Cemetery to enjoy our well-deserved snack and drink.

For some reason, Cpl. J. R. did not want to stop at our usual place this afternoon. Instead, he seemed to be distracted and was pulling me to go in a different direction. I gave in and let him lead me. He appeared to be on a mission and was making a beeline toward

Charles Patrick's Cpl. J. R. Dugan

another bench that we had never used before. I was becoming concerned at his wild behavior. Today, he suddenly appeared to be obsessed with getting to a destination known only to him.

When we arrived at the bench, I sat down and let Cpl. J. R. have a lot of leash. He started scratching at a grave that had been covered by years of dirt, leaves, and neglect. I watched in amazement, as this was the only grave that I have ever seen him scratch at like this. He frantically threw dirt in every direction. I became worried that there might be something beneath the leaves that could hurt him, so I stood up to rein him in.

As I walked behind him, my interest was piqued when I saw that

Cpl. J. R. had been digging at a military gravestone. He turned and looked at me as if to ask for my assistance. I got down on my knees and began to scrape the dirt and debris away from the stone. As I reached the surface of the stone and my hand swept the final layer away, Cpl. J. R. stopped. Rigidly, he stared at the stone. My head turned away from Cpl. J. R., and I looked at the tombstone. I could not breathe, and my heart pounded as I read the tombstone's inscription:

JACK A. RUSSELL

TEXAS

CPL SIGNAL CORPS

JULY 21, 1928 – JULY 16, 1952

I was speechless. It seemed as if all time and motion had frozen. A sudden chill ran up my spine. Cpl. J. R. laid his head on both paws and rested on the headstone of Cpl. Jack Russell, a soldier with his own name, who had been killed in the Korean War. The poor condition of the soldier's grave site indicated that this was a man who was not being remembered by friends, family, or lovers. But somehow, Cpl. Jack A. Russell had a link to my little dog. Cpl. J. R. and I both sat for a long time, paying our respects to this man who had served his country and made the ultimate sacrifice in time of war.

While we lingered at Cpl. Russell's grave, I tried to gather my wits as to what had just happened. It was amazing to be part of an experience that had joined all of us together in a brief moment in time and eternity.

Later, Cpl. J. R. and I cleaned the grave site and tombstone of

Cpl. Jack A. Russell, to make it a visible and very important part of this world again. I continue to marvel at how, on this day so near to November's Veterans Day, a little dog paid honor and respect by bringing new meaning to the belief that no soldier should ever be forgotten.

Meditation

Has a dog remembered and showed honor to you, a loved one, or even a stranger in a way that surprised you?

An Angel in the Night

Diana Johnson
Plano, Texas
as told to Mary J. Yerkes
Manassas, Virginia

*W*ith the long, dark winter finally behind us, a brisk March wind ushered in spring — and on its heels, an angel in the night came to live with us.

A sudden gust of wind caught the bottom of his coat as my husband, Forrest, carefully tucked Lauren, the youngest of our five children, into the baby's car seat. The wind was unusually bad, making our short drive to the airport difficult. From the passenger's seat, I watched as Forrest's knuckles gripped the top of the steering wheel. He fought to keep our minivan from drifting into the next lane. It seemed a fitting metaphor to describe the past year — a real white-knuckle ride!

Our youngest twins, Lauren and Branden, were born eight weeks premature. Within minutes of her birth, Lauren, the smaller of the two, had stopped breathing. In the hospital, I watched in horror as her tiny pink lips turned blue. She was quickly resuscitated, whisked off to the neonatal intensive care unit, and placed on a ventilator. Branden didn't fare much better. A month later, Lauren and Branden, both on apnea monitors, came home to meet their brother

26

and sisters. The older twins, Brianna and little Forrest, were three, and Taylor was two. We quickly established a routine. Within weeks, we were ready to welcome yet another new member of the family, Zeke. We didn't think that our family would be complete without a dog! So we were on our way on this windy night to bring him home.

At the airport, I leaned over to Forrest and whispered, "What if it doesn't work out? Zeke's two years old and probably set in his ways. What if he can't adjust?"

"The breeder was sure he would, Diana," Forrest reminded me.

I had searched long and hard for a responsible collie breeder before I found Susan. After I explained that we have five children — two with serious health problems — she wisely steered us away from a puppy.

"Diana," Susan said when I called her, "I have a two-year-old champion collie. Zeke will be perfect for your family. He's a beautiful tricolor and a true collie in every sense. He loves life, and he especially loves children."

Even though I had my heart set on having a puppy, with Susan's recommendation, I agreed to give Zeke a try.

Now my thoughts were interrupted by a high-pitched squeal. "Zeke's here!" announced Brianna. An attendant ushered us to a large crate, where I saw a long nose pushed up against the wire with a mass of ebony and white fur behind it. After speaking a few reassuring words to Zeke, I nodded to the attendant and said, "We're ready."

Zeke inched his way out, looking cautious yet curious. Within seconds, my animal lover Brianna threw her tiny arms around Zeke's neck, buried her face in his long fur, and murmured, "I love you,

Diana's Zeke with Lauren

Zeke." Little Forrest added, "We're your new family. Welcome home!"

Zeke quickly settled in to his new life with us. We arranged his bed in the master bedroom. But right from the start, Zeke made it clear that he preferred sleeping in the nursery between the babies' cribs. There was barely room to move with five oxygen canisters, a suction machine, and all of the other medical equipment in the room. But the nurse who helped us care for the twins didn't mind, so I decided to let Zeke stay with her and the infants.

One night, about three weeks after his arrival, Zeke jumped up on my side of the bed and thwacked me with his paw. I glanced at the clock; it was 3:30 A.M. "Go back to sleep, Zeke," I murmured. Zeke refused to take no for an answer. Instead, he ran barking back and forth between my side of the bed and the door.

"Shhhhh . . . you'll wake the children," I chided as I got up, thinking he probably had to go out. I headed to the back door, but Zeke wouldn't follow. Barking, he turned and ran in the opposite direction.

"Zeke, come," I called. Annoyed, I shuffled down the hall after him into the nursery. Why isn't he listening? I wondered. "Zeke, come," I called again. It's useless, I thought and resigned myself to the fact that I would just need to lead him out by his collar. I watched as Zeke jumped up with his paws on Lauren's crib rail. I placed two fingers under his collar and casually glanced down at Lauren. *Oh my God! She's not breathing!*

I yanked Lauren's lifeless body from the crib as I screamed, "Forrest, call 911!" The baby hung in my arms like a rag doll. I frantically blew the first rescue breath past her blue lips. Her saliva tasted salty as it mingled with the tears streaming down my face. Suddenly, I heard a choking sound. I quickly turned Lauren over to clear her airway. When I turned her back toward me, she started to cry.

"She's breathing!" I exclaimed, relief flooding my body.

"Why didn't the monitor go off?" Forrest asked the nurse. After examining the monitor more closely, Forrest had his answer. He turned to the nurse and said, "The wires are crossed." Furious, I punched the nursing agency number into the phone while we waited for the ambulance to arrive. Within minutes, we were given a new nurse. When the paramedics arrived, they checked Lauren over. "She looks like she's doing fine now," one of them said. "You got to her just in time."

At the hospital the next morning, Lauren was given a battery of tests. There was no permanent damage. Thank God! It was a miracle. Exhausted and relieved, we took Lauren home. Zeke greeted us at the front door.

"Zeke, what would we have done without you?" I asked.

I carried Lauren, who had fallen asleep in the car, into the nursery. Zeke followed closely behind and watched as I laid Lauren in her crib. Satisfied that she was fine, Zeke contentedly plopped onto the rug in his usual spot next to Lauren's crib.

Forrest turned to me and asked, "Do you think the baby will be all right?"

I glanced at Zeke and replied, "She'll be fine."

Meditation

Has a dog persisted in letting you know that you or someone else is in danger or needs assistance?

Lee County Prisoners Give Life to Death Row Dogs

Jay Williams

Fort Myers, Florida

I got involved with the Lee County Cell Dogs Program in early October 2004 as an inmate at the minimum-security section of the Community Programs Unit at Lee County Stockade Annex in Fort Myers, Florida. To understand the bond between people and dogs, you have to have had a dog. In my childhood, I was practically raised around dogs, so I relate to them and they relate to me. The Cell Dogs Program appealed to me because I wanted the chance to find out where learning to train dogs could lead me. I also suspected that I'd have to develop patience. By the time I volunteered for the program, I had figured out that patience is the key to everything.

With high hopes that I'd at last have something I was successful at, I applied for the program along with fifty-six other inmates. I made it through the first cut, and twenty-six of us had our records screened to make sure there was no past violence toward people or animals. I was one of the fourteen inmates finally chosen to participate in the program.

Our Cell Dogs Program is a partnership between Lee County

Animal Services and the Lee County Sheriff's Office. Sheriff's Captain Tom Weaver, Commander of Community Programs at the prison, saw a television show about cell dogs and decided to launch a program with the inmates in our facility. He thought that the inmates and dogs would have positive effects on one another.

Was he ever right about that! Today, our Cell Dogs Program is so successful that it has become a model for others. People contact Captain Weaver from all over the country and ask to come to Lee County to watch inmates and dogs in action and learn how the program operates.

Animal Services provides the dogs' food, kennel crates, and veterinary services. We inmates give the dogs training in obedience, socialization, and basic commands. Homeless dogs, who may be on their last chance, destined for death row and facing euthanization, live with inmate-trainers and sleep in crates beside our beds with one to two dogs in each unit. We train the dogs every day during the course and are their full-time companions.

The dogs who graduate from our program are highly adoptable, having learned how to heel, sit, stay, and recall, which is a command for the dog to come back to the trainer. The dogs are also house-trained, leash-trained, and taught to respond to voice commands and some hand signals. The Cell Dogs Program provides the inmates with job skills in dog training, dog grooming, and veterinary assistance.

In October 2004, I became the primary trainer for a female black Labrador–beagle mix. For the first six weeks of the program, Brent, a fellow inmate, was my backup trainer.

The Obstacles

Because of her dark-chocolate coloring, I decided to name the dog Hershey. I knew very little about her. Either Hershey's people gave her up because of bad behavior, or the animal control shelter in Fort Myers found her on the street as a stray. I also didn't know Hershey's age, but the program's professional dog trainers estimated that she was about a year and a half old.

Even though I didn't have much history about Hershey, after she came into my care, I soon figured out what life must have been like for her. When I first saw Hershey, I thought that she looked like one of those untrained dogs who do anything they want to. However, I noticed that every time I tried to pet, hold, or carry her, Hershey acted frightened. Hershey's rib cage was showing, because she was so thin from not eating. I concluded that this dog must have been abused.

I said, "Oh boy, we have a lot of work to do to make her into a good dog!" But like the other inmates in our Cell Dogs Program, I had only eight weeks to train her into a dog that people would be glad to adopt.

The regular dog-training classes took place each Wednesday. The rest of the week, it was up to the other inmate trainers and me to prove that the dogs could be trained. We had to demonstrate that the Cell Dogs Program was worth the time and money Lee County was putting into it.

I hoped that Hershey would pass the training program with flying colors, but because of her fear of being touched and how scrawny she looked, I wasn't sure if this dog could make it. The entire training program wouldn't stop because of one dog's failure, but my part in the program would end if there were too many problems with Hershey.

I faced another challenge in training Hershey. I've been deaf all of my life. Being deaf isn't as bad as people think it is. There are some advantages. For example, I can sleep through heavy rainstorms. I can't hear when someone is yapping at me. I don't have to listen to people's baloney talk. The only disadvantage is that there is no music for me. Other than small drawbacks to being deaf, I live a normal life just like others do every day. I was soon to find out, though, if being deaf would make it hard for me to train Hershey.

For the first two weeks, I was really worried how Hershey would respond to my methods. Fortunately, it turned out that the fact that I am deaf didn't make it harder for me to train her. It actually made it easier. I'm used to using sign language and communicating with my hands. Giving hand signals to Hershey came naturally to me. If I raised my hand and placed it in front of her face, this was the signal for Hershey to obey the *stay* command. When I started bending my hand down, she was supposed to sit. I don't think Hershey ever knew that I was deaf. Since she is such a smart dog, she probably wondered, though, why I was doing things differently than the other trainers, who mostly used their voices to train the dogs.

Hershey Makes Progress

After the initial two-week period of training, I began to see some development in Hershey. Instead of being hyper or moving around a lot, she was making eye contact with me. She began looking directly at my hands or at me, and I could see that she was learning to pay attention. Once, during our training, I mistakenly and abruptly stopped walking. Hershey sat down and waited patiently. It was as if she were showing that she had confidence in whatever I did or asked her to do, even if it was out of the ordinary. That's when I relaxed, sensing that Hershey trusted me to help her become a good dog for someone.

I didn't like to work Hershey too hard, so sometimes we had break days. We would take it easy, and I'd let her enjoy some freedom. On break days, the inmates let all the dogs in the program run around in the front yard of the stockade compound. I encouraged Hershey to play with the other dogs. Surprisingly, even when the dogs wanted to play, run, chase, or be chased by her, Hershey kept close to me. Her choice to stay near made it obvious that Hershey and I had become a team.

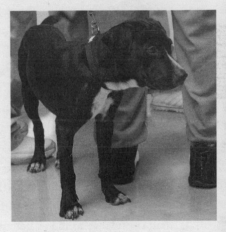

Jay's Cell Dog Hershey

A couple of weeks into Hershey's training, Captain Weaver took Hershey to the vet for her shots and to be checked for worms. He told me later that Hershey had enjoyed riding in his car. Since Hershey came to me as a skinny, scared, and abused dog, I felt really good that she was beginning to look and act more and more like an average dog — one who liked to poke her head out of a car window and see the world.

I liked seeing Hershey's progress not only in obeying the commands but also in her emotions. At first, she had been scared whenever I tried to pet her. If I waved my arms around, she'd duck as if she thought I would hit her. But by now, she was responding to all the love I was giving her. I was happy that she was always excited to see me. When I'd bring her out of the crate, she'd jump up on me, no longer fearful at all.

When we were about three weeks into the training, I noticed that Hershey was responding much better to me than my own dogs at home had done. Even so, she did not exactly act as if she thought of herself as *my* dog. I sensed a sort of loving detachment in her. It made me wonder if somehow Hershey knew that our relationship was temporary.

The teacher of our Cell Dogs Program, Coralie Rumbold, and her three assistants, Terry, Luann, and Jean, were telling me that Hershey had become the best of all the dogs in our training class. Coralie also said that Hershey was one of the calmer dogs — focused and alert. The teacher's comments made me feel great, because some of the dogs were hyper, kind of unfocused, and always wiggling around. They just couldn't settle down and stay in one spot.

I am good with dogs, and Hershey may have sensed that and had confidence in me as her trainer. I think that Hershey did exercises well because she knew she would receive praise from me and maybe a doggy biscuit, too. Hershey, like other dogs, became happy when she heard excited voices. Although I used hand signals for her training, she could hear the excitement in my voice when she did something well.

Reaching the Halfway Mark

As the weeks progressed, I worked on getting Hershey to go where I wanted her to go and do what I wanted her to do. For one of the training exercises, I would place a towel on the floor and take Hershey about two yards away from it. Then I used a hand signal and said, "Place." Off she would go to the towel and lie down until I signaled for her to come back to me. Perfecto! Everyone liked that discipline in her, because this exercise helps the people who adopt a dog from our program. If the dog has done something wrong, the person can say, "Place," and the dog will go back to where she sleeps and stay there until the person lets her come out and join the family again. Sort of a way to give dogs a time-out for bad behavior.

I was becoming more and more proud of Hershey. By week four of the training, she knew the hand signals telling her to sit, lie down, and stay. She understood the *come* and *heel* commands. She also had mastered the *place* hand signals. To me, this was impressive. Most dogs have the hardest time with *stay*. Hershey knew *stay* before any of the other dogs even started to comprehend what that command meant.

As we got closer to Hershey's graduation from the Cell Dogs Program, she had to do different things to show she'd be adoptable. Captain Weaver took her away from jail one day to his house to find out if Hershey could get along with his cats. After the captain's wife, Nancy Weaver, took Hershey for this pet "test drive," she said that Hershey had enjoyed riding in the car from jail to her house and back to the jail. I thought, "Good luck to Hershey!"

The day that Hershey went to visit Captain and Mrs. Weaver and their cats, I knew Hershey would come back to me, so it was not too hard on me to have her gone all day. After all, Hershey and I had been together 24/7 for a long time. So it was kind of like getting a break, like having a babysitter take care of your kids for a day, as long as you know it is only for one day. If the time away were for more than a day, it would break your heart, big time. I guess this day away with the Weavers helped to prepare me for when Hershey would leave me to live in her new home.

When Captain Weaver returned Hershey to me, I was very happy to have her back. Mrs. Weaver had a nice time with Hershey and said that the dog ended the day by sleeping in the bed with her. Mrs. Weaver thought that she might want to adopt Hershey. This got my hopes up. I'd sleep better knowing that Hershey was in good hands and had been adopted by nice and loving people. But later, I was disappointed to find out the Weavers would not be adopting Hershey after all. This meant that I had to go through the anxiety of wondering what kind of home Hershey would find after our training ended.

Would Hershey Graduate?

At last, it was time for Hershey to go to the Cell Dogs show, where hundreds of people would come to see the dogs. On the day of the show, I paced around, not knowing if anyone had liked or wanted Hershey. Later, Mrs. Weaver and the teacher's assistants told me that attendance at the show had been good and that Hershey had done fine. Now that she was all trained and ready to go, it would be only a few days before she was put up for adoption. That's when I really started worrying about her. I wondered if people would want dogs from jail who had been trained by felons or convicted criminals.

One day, one of the prison guards, Officer Daniello, gave me a really big Ziploc bag full of treats for Hershey. That bag lasted for the days remaining until graduation/adoption day, which would be on December 1, 2004. Being able to reward Hershey with the treats helped both the dog and me. I wrote up a report and made sure the Lee County Jail recognized Officer Daniello for her good heart in giving dog treats for Hershey out of her own pocket. God bless her.

Right before Hershey and I parted, I fed her but forgot to lock her kennel door before I left for my own chow line. When I returned to our tent, Hershey was sitting on my bed waiting for me! Wow! She could have run around and made a mess of everything, but she hadn't. All she did was just lie down on my bed, being a good dog. That amazed everyone. We could see that Hershey had really matured and was truly ready to become someone's wonderful pet.

In the remaining days we had together, Hershey and I practiced the things we were supposed to do for the graduation ceremony. She had to pass ten portions of the American Kennel Association's tests. She needed to do things like accept being petted by friendly people, not show aggressiveness, walk easily among other dogs, obey basic commands, and tolerate being groomed and examined. After graduation, Hershey would qualify as an American Kennel Association "Canine Good Citizen."

Hershey's graduation day was one that I wanted to last forever. I wasn't nervous at all, though, because I knew Hershey would do a good job. She proved me right. Hershey was wonderful!

Would Hershey Find a Home?

People who were considering adopting the dogs from our program attended the graduation ceremony. To my relief, Frank and Leigh Ann Gibson adopted Hershey on the spot. I'm a pretty good judge of people. By looking at the Gibsons, seeing how they were dressed, and watching how they related to their children and to Hershey, I could tell that they were a good working family. They looked like people who made a decent living and would take care of the dog. From what I could see, the Gibsons were good people and Hershey was going to the right kind of home.

The experiences with Hershey stayed with me long after her graduation and adoption, especially the patience and kindness that I developed while training this loving dog. As part of the Cell Dogs Program, the primary trainer writes a letter about the dog to the people who adopted her. My advice to Hershey's new family was simple. I wrote, "Hershey is a mix of Labrador and beagle. Basically she is a very calm dog, very good at getting along with anyone who wants to command her. You will love to have her in your possession. She is a gentle dog to be with. She likes to sleep in bed with you. Please take extra good care of Hershey. God and Jesus, bless us all."

I was surprised and felt totally blessed at how Hershey and I developed our relationship into such bonding. What was so great for both Hershey and me was the closeness that we had with each other. It's hard to explain exactly how Hershey and I became fast friends. At first, she was someone to get used to. After a few days together, we began to trust each other and form a friendship. Sometimes, animals seem to give that friendship better than humans do.

I used to think that I'd always be a failure, having been in jail.

Then, with Hershey, I saw myself succeeding. Now I know I can have success if I am motivated and have the patience to stay through everything. Today, as I come close to my release from prison, I am seriously considering going back to school to learn auto-body repair. I want to feel success again. It's a good feeling!

I know that there won't ever be another dog like Hershey. I truly miss her. I wish I could see her for one last time and watch how well she is doing. All I can say is that when you have a dog like Hershey in your life, you are truly blessed for that close kind of bond that you won't find anywhere else.

Meditation

When have you had to honor the greater good for a dog or a person and pass along a blessing that you would love to have kept for yourself?

Postscript from Cell Dog Hershey

Frank and Leigh Ann Gibson
Lehigh Acres, Florida

*A*dopting Hershey was more than a simple process of filling out paperwork. Before we could take Hershey home, Lee County Animal Services and the Lee County Sheriff's Office were thorough in checking on the backgrounds of those who wanted to adopt the cell dogs. They made sure that none of us had had problems with previous pets. They also checked with our regular veterinarians to find out if our current and previous pets were up to date on shots and vet visits and whether we were the kind of people who took good care of animals. They asked us questions such as how long the pet would be alone during the day. They were very careful to make sure the dogs would be placed in loving homes.

The Cell Dogs Program graduation ceremony was filled with pomp and circumstance. It turned into a real tearjerker to watch the graduates proudly walk out with their inmate trainers and fulfill the requirements for becoming an American Kennel Association "Canine Good Citizen."

After the demonstration, testing, and ceremony, we spent an hour with Jay Williams, talking with him through an interpreter, since Jay is deaf. We were impressed with Jay. Jay told us that Hershey was very smart and trainable. He said that she was intelligent enough and had the temperament to be trained as a service dog. Our only concern was that we would be taking Hershey away and how hard this would be on him. The teachers said that everyone knew the training period was for eight weeks. Jay and his assistant trainer would be getting new dogs to train the very next day.

We adopted Hershey and brought her into our home on December 1, 2004. Hershey was a little hesitant leaving the stockade the night of the adoptions, so much so that we had to pick her up and put her in the car. She wasn't aggressive, but obviously she was nervous, leaving the familiar surroundings where she had received so much love from Jay.

When we arrived home, our nine-pound rat terrier enthusiasti-

Frank and Leigh Ann's Hershey

cally greeted Hershey. Since then, the two dogs have formed an amazing bond. They play hard and then nap together.

We are so happy with what a wonderful dog Hershey is; she's the best! Hershey is a very loving dog and the most compassionate of any pet we have ever had. She seems to be sensitive to her surroundings, knowing what activity is appropriate for the moment. When our boys are doing homework, she stays quietly by their feet. But if there is free time to play with them, she is ready to go.

Hershey slept with her trainer in the Cell Dogs Program, which is tight sleeping quarters. She obviously got used to the companionship.

Since coming to live with us, Hershey sleeps with one of our boys each night, never leaving his side until morning.

Each one of us feels that we are Hershey's favorite, but she shows us all much love and apparently appreciates her new home. Hershey is very lucky to have the second chance she received from the Lee County Sheriff's Office Cell Dogs Program. But we are even luckier to have adopted her into our family.

Meditation

Has a dog come from an unusual source and brought happiness into your life in ways for which you are eternally grateful?

Note: For more information about the Lee County Sheriff's Office Cell Dogs Program, visit www.leelostpets.com.

A Puppy's Love Prepared Me
for Motherhood

Jill Kelly
Alpharetta, Georgia

*S*ince I was getting past the age of thirty-five and had been recently separated from my husband, I wondered if I would ever become a parent. If I did have that opportunity, would I be a good mother? I had babysat only twice in my life, and both times were for kids who were five or six years old and potty trained. They could tell me what they wanted or needed. I didn't have any experience taking care of helpless babies. I also had never cared for our family's dogs. Just prior to this time while I lived alone and was wondering if children would be in my future, someone gave me a six-week-old puppy. So, here I was, alone, only responsible for taking care of myself and a small animal. How hard could "motherhood" be?

I was soon to find out.

You might think that paper-training the puppy or having my slippers chewed up would be my biggest adjustments. But I discovered that the hardest part of having a newborn puppy was being away from her. Elle', my little fawn-and-white boxer mix, suddenly became the reason I got out of bed in the morning, because she had to go out. Elle' was also the reason I came home every two or three hours, since she had to go out or to eat. I snuggled up to her every night, and this little bundle of fur even gave me my 1998 New Year's Eve kiss.

I found myself thinking about Elle' all the time. I had to remember her doctors' appointments. I made sure she went on walks. Of course, she had to have the best food and lots of fun toys. I took her everywhere — the bank, the cleaners, and anywhere else that had a drive-through service. We would drive to PETsMART for shopping. Then we *had* to pull up to the Sonic restaurant's window and order our treats. While Elle' chomped on a cup of ice, I'd drink a Diet Vanilla Coke.

Jill's Elle' and Emeril Boudreax

If my friends wanted me to come over, most of them were sweet enough to say, "Sure, you can bring Elle'," although they probably really didn't need another dog at their houses for the afternoon, especially since my puppy was a wild little thing. After a while, I realized that Elle' had become the reason I wasn't thinking about the other challenges I faced. Anxiety over what was happening in my life would have probably paralyzed my world. Instead, while I took care of Elle', she was really taking care of me. No doubt she was the best thing that could have happened to me during that time of insecurity and indecision.

As I fast-forward to today, I am happy to say that my husband and I reconciled, probably because we both had responsibility for Elle' during our separation. Caring for her gave us a new perspective on how happy we could be, sharing our life's experiences together. In June 2000, Emeril, another boxer, joined our family. And in May 2003, our baby boy, Jack, was born.

Having a human baby has helped me to understand how taking care of Elle's' doctors' appointments, shopping for her food, and picking out great toys had transformed a woman with no previous responsibility for a baby into a better mother for Jack. Elle' taught me to ask the important questions: Is the baby warm enough? Does he have enough to eat? Is he getting lots of kisses every day?

As I take the three of us — Jack, Elle', and Emeril — for walks every day, I think about all the ways Elle', in her doggy way, made me realize that it's nice to have a reason to come home every night. And it's wonderful to have someone to love, to take care of, and to kiss every New Year's Eve. Adopting Elle' and having the responsibility for her care, along with all the love she gave, prepared me for motherhood. I'll always be grateful to her. And someday, maybe my son will thank her too.

Meditation

What responsibilities has caring for a puppy prepared you to accept? Could a puppy help you learn your capabilities and limitations?

Temujin's Spiritual Message

Sun Lakes, Arizona

*S*everal years ago, I was at a point when I felt that something was keeping me from achieving my spiritual goals. Throughout my adult life, I had always wanted to be more aware of the Holy Spirit and to let go of all my worries and concerns about the future. I had the true desire to relax and allow Spirit to guide me in every part of my life. While my career and other parts of my life were going well, in another, deeper part of myself, I didn't seem to be growing. Deep inside, I felt out of harmony with Spirit. Consequently, I was anxious about some changes that I'd soon have to make. My anxieties were stopping me from reaching the elusive goal I'd set for my spiritual unfoldment of fully trusting Spirit.

At that time, we lived near the edge of the desert outside of Phoenix, Arizona. Whenever I felt down about anything, my remedy was to go for a long walk in the desert with my special dog, Temujin. He loved taking long desert strolls with me.

Temujin was a mastiff with brindle coloring. He weighed in at about 150 pounds of solid love. Everyone who ever met this dog felt his boundless joy for all life. He played with each person or dog he met. He'd catch and chase balls and wrestle with contagious enthusiasm that made everyone who watched him laugh.

One of Temujin's special treats, when accompanying me on desert walks, was to find treasures to proudly show off. He'd dance around me with his find of the day — sometimes a stick, more often parts of small trees. Because of his size, he could carry back just about anything that to him seemed worthwhile. We put a huge box near the door of our house to store the treasures Temujin brought home.

One day, while I was thinking about the lack of progress in my spiritual growth, Temujin and I walked in a very remote part of the desert. Temujin wandered off on his quest for treasure, while I ambled alone, deep in thought. Again and again, I kept going over every aspect of my life, wondering what was holding me back spiritually.

With a heavy heart, finally, in total frustration, I stopped, looked up to the sky, and pleaded aloud for an answer from the Holy Spirit. Feeling desperate, I called out, "What do I need? How can I learn to trust?"

Within a few seconds, here came Temujin, heading straight for me with the newest treasure in his mouth. I wasn't paying much attention to him, since I had so many troubles on my mind. Temujin stopped directly in front of me and dropped his gift at my feet. This was quite unusual, because his usual game was to dance all around and play keep-away with me, as he guarded his treasure.

Today, instead of hiding it, he sat down, looked me straight in the eye, gazed down at his find, and then looked up at me again. My curiosity aroused, I followed Temujin's eyes and saw a black-and-red baseball cap on the ground. Of course, the first thing I did was look all around, trying to figure out where this dog could have possibly picked up a baseball cap in the middle of the desert. But we were entirely alone out there. Again, Temujin looked up at me, then at the hat, and back to me.

Wayne's Temujin as a puppy

I picked up the baseball hat and examined it. In big red letters were two words: *No Fear.* Temujin focused on me and then, once more, stared at the baseball hat in my hand. "No fear," I said. Temujin's huge tail started wagging, noisily thumping the ground, as I kept repeating the words: *No Fear.*

At last, I realized that Temujin had delivered the answer to my spiritual question about how to take the next step on my spiritual journey. The answer was, no fear.

That's when I realized that I had been allowing numerous small fears and worries to overwhelm me. I had become tense instead of relaxing enough to let Divine Spirit work out the obstacles in my path.

In that moment of recognition, a huge weight lifted from my heart. I began laughing out loud at the message — and at the unique messenger. Now, quite satisfied that he had delivered the answer to my question, Temujin trotted away a few feet, as I stood, still laughing at the hat in my hand. Then he suddenly stopped, looked around at me, gave a big snort, and vigorously shook his head with an expression of disdain. He must have been amazed at how long it had taken me to get the very clear message from Spirit. His life was truly an example of having absolutely no fear and living in the moment with love and joy. My slowness at understanding had tested his patience.

I still have the hat that says *No Fear*. When life's challenges become too much, I always remember its motto. Perhaps my greatest lesson in life is to trust the Holy Spirit, knowing that divine love helps and protects me in every aspect of life. All I must do is have no fear. Whenever I have a problem or challenge, I now never hesitate to ask for an answer. And I am no longer surprised at the messenger Spirit guides to deliver it.

Meditation

If Temujin presented you with a cap from the lonely desert and it said *No Fear*, how would you interpret this message in your life? When has a canine divine messenger delivered the answer you've been looking for?

Casey: A Warrior of the Heart Brings Love to a Nursing Home

Pat Eisenberger
Warren, Michigan

*W*hen a sheltie (Shetland sheepdog) chooses a human companion, he or she will stick with the person through thick and thin. Some shelties see no reason to acknowledge the presence of anyone other than their chosen person, except to warn them to keep away. So I was shocked when one day my sheltie, Casey, joyfully ran over to an elderly couple he did not know. He danced about them and cuddled up for their attention, ignoring me as I called for him to come back.

After that incident, I began carefully watching Casey's behavior around other people. Casey didn't care for strangers who were in their twenties, thirties, or forties, and he even ran away from children. But let someone with gray hair walk by, and Casey ran to greet him or her enthusiastically. Since this was not typical sheltie behavior, I began to think that maybe Casey was intended to accomplish something greater with his life. And maybe I could help him.

I contacted my church's nursing home and found out that they welcomed anyone, including dogs, to visit the residents. I felt confident that Casey could brighten the day for many of the people at this facility, but I was uncertain how I could handle taking him there. Most of the residents of this nursing home were Alzheimer's patients. How could Casey and I communicate with them? I had been observing Casey become so much more than his sheltie temperament dictated. I hoped that I, too, could step outside my comfort level and try to bring a little joy to people in the nursing home who needed it. So I arranged for Casey and me to make our first visit to the elderly.

The minute Casey stepped into the nursing home, people greeted us with smiles and laughter. Casey happily did his tricks for them. He stayed at the end of the hall until I called him, then came barreling around past people in wheelchairs. Having this furry bullet bolt by made them laugh. He sat, laid down, rolled over, crawled, weaved through my legs as I walked, and caught his tennis ball. After Casey finished entertaining the patients, he wagged his tail, cuddled up, and listened to his elders, especially when they called him "pretty dog." Casey accepted every hand that reached out to him with a friendly lick and a wag of his tail.

Pat's Casey

The next thing I knew, people who couldn't tell where they were or even who they were began to glow with a light in their eyes and reminisce about the dogs they had loved. When a nurse saw that one old gent had started talking to Casey, she pulled me aside and whispered, "He hasn't said a word since he got here — until now!"

Someone else asked me to take Casey to a woman who was unable to move from her bed or even speak. As the woman petted Casey's head and hummed at him, I observed indications of a sharp and active mind behind her bright eyes. She happily responded to my questions with a smile and a nod or an elegant wave of her hand.

I left the nursing home that day feeling very grateful to Casey for the lesson he had taught me. I had been afraid to step outside the boundaries I had placed around myself and worried about how I would communicate with these people. But I learned that no one ever forgets the language of love. Casey and I continued visiting nursing homes for another two years until Casey retired from this form of service.

Casey and I would like to challenge you to step outside your boundaries. We think that you'll find the experience to be awesome!

Meditation

How is the dog in your life showing you his or her true purpose? Are you paying attention to the signals?

They're Still Walking

Bill Mann
Madison, Tennessee

*W*hen my father retired in 1989, he and Mom moved from their home in Tampa, Florida, to the mountains of western North Carolina, north of Asheville. For exercise, Dad would walk six to eight miles a day in the mountains surrounding their new home. On one of his walks, he saw an Australian shepherd–cattle dog mix who was all tangled up in the chain that was intended to keep him in his yard. Dad went over and untangled him and also refilled his overturned water bowl. From that day on, Dad and this dog became friends, and Dad would always stop to say hello on his daily walks.

Once, a few minutes after Dad passed by, the dog broke his chain and followed him on his walk. Dad brought the dog back to his human companion, who thanked him and chained up the dog again. After that, the dog would regularly break his chain and find Dad wherever he could. He'd come down to my parents' home and sit on their deck, staring in at Dad through the sliding glass doors. Since this was someone else's dog, Dad made a point of never letting him in the house or feeding him. He would eventually walk the dog the half-mile back to his home. Still, the dog kept coming to visit, regardless of the weather. Once, he sat on the deck for hours, in two feet of snow, until Dad finally put on his coat and boots and took him back home.

Finally our neighbor said to Dad, "You might as well keep that dog. I think he loves you more than us."

So Dad and Mom adopted the dog and named him Aussie. But his nickname was "The Love Hound."

Dad sat in a big easy chair, and Aussie would lie at his feet, staring at my father until finally Dad gave in and scratched his head. It

Bill and Aussie

was amusing to watch this sixty-five-pound dog trying to sneak up into Dad's lap, one paw at a time.

Dad and Aussie went on walks together almost every day for several years. Then one day, Dad was diagnosed with terminal liver cancer and told that he had six to twelve months to live. My wife, Deborah, my mom, and I drove Dad to Florida so he could have access to treatment at a cancer research center there. My father told us that he had been dealing with pain and nausea for a year or more but hadn't wanted to bother anyone about it.

While Dad's health continued to decline, Aussie stayed under his bed, right beneath him. Throughout the rest of Dad's life, including when he was no longer able to get up, Aussie never left him. The dog's sadness was palpable. He ate very little. After we'd take him out to do his business, he would immediately return to his post with

Dad. Only ten weeks after his diagnosis, Dad passed away, with Aussie lying quietly under his bed.

After Dad's passing, Aussie definitely went through a period of mourning. He was clearly not his old, energetic self. But in time, he seemed to accept that Dad was gone, and much of his enthusiasm for life returned. But he never forgot Dad.

A few weeks after Dad's death, Deborah, Mom, and I returned to North Carolina. We scattered Dad's ashes along the trails he loved to walk. And Aussie came to live with us. Although we loved him a great deal, none of us could spend as much time with the dog as Dad had.

Several months after Dad's death, we were cleaning out a closet in the basement and found a life-size black-and-white photograph cutout of Dad that had been mounted on cardboard. It was left over from some event related to Dad's coaching career at the University of South Florida, in Tampa. We set it out as a kind of impromptu memorial to him. Not too long afterward, we discovered Aussie, his tail wagging joyfully, looking up at the poster with what could only be described as hopeful anticipation. He kept a vigil by that poster until we put it away again.

About a year and a half after Dad left us, our situation changed, and we had to find a new home for Aussie. My brother, Michael, suggested one of his former students, who lived in Florida and had an Australian shepherd who needed companionship. Fortunately, this family was eager to adopt Aussie.

About a month before the new family was to adopt him, we noticed that Aussie seemed to be experiencing some pain. He wasn't limping at all; he would just start yelping loudly and approach one of us in a submissive position, with his head down and his tail between his legs. At first we thought something must have attacked him, but that wasn't the case. In retrospect, we think these were signs of a worsening condition that affected his range of motion. Our local vet said the pain was probably due to a bone spur and pre-scribed what he called "canine ibuprofen," which seemed to help Aussie feel better.

The day after Aussie arrived in Florida to live in his new home, he experienced a recurrence of the pain. His new family took him to their vet, where X-rays revealed that Aussie had advanced spinal cancer. Two of his vertebrae had deteriorated beyond repair. Aussie would have to be euthanized to end his pain. This family responded with a great deal of compassion. Before we could even offer to pay for the vet, they said they would take care of the bill. They took com-plete responsibility, as if Aussie were an old family friend. It was very gracious of them.

I really loved Aussie and seriously considered driving to Florida to be with him physically for this final appointment, but because of my work, I just wasn't able to do it. At the exact time when Aussie was scheduled to leave his physical body, I sat alone in silent con-templation, so I could at least be with him spiritually. With my eyes closed, I visualized Aussie lying on a stainless-steel table. As I bent over to nuzzle him, he lifted his head and licked my face as if to say, "It's okay. I love you too."

Deborah and I couldn't help but notice the similarities be-tween Dad's and Aussie's deaths. Cancer had taken them both. And like Dad, Aussie hadn't told us about his pain until it was too late to save him. They both ended up traveling to Florida to die. It was clear to us that Dad and Aussie had a very deep and special bond. I'm sure that to this day, wherever they are, they're still taking those long walks together.

I'm a songwriter, and the day after Aussie left us, I wrote a song called "They're Still Walking." Its lyrics told the story of the special relationship between Dad and Aussie. Wherever I sing it, people are deeply touched. Perhaps it makes them remember the loyal friendships they have had with dogs in their own lives. To this day, "They're Still Walking" is one of my most-requested songs.

Meditation

Has there been a time when a dog's companionship and unconditional love allowed you to live a fuller life? Is there a special dog companion who shared your emotional and physical health challenges?

Ask Taylor

Dear Taylor,

My dog follows me everywhere. She doesn't let me out
of her sight. Is she worried about me? Or does she
find me endlessly fascinating? No one has ever been
that into me.

Sincerely,
Boring to Everybody but My Dog

Dear Boring,

You are the most delightful and interesting person
in the world to your dog companion. She adores your
every move and will be there just in case you need
some extra loving or emotional support.

Besides, you are the source of her fondest
desires -- food, kisses, and snuggles, in that
order.

Always into you,

Taylor

Are dogs God's furry heroes? In the next chapter you will meet the angel dog heroes who save lives and serve those who need the help of perceptive and skillful animal friends.

CHAPTER TWO

What If Heroes Have Four Paws and Fur?

Spiritually if you want to have a role model and don't want to look to other people or a Master, look to dogs. Dogs have a good relationship with life, generally.

— Harold Klemp, *Animals Are Soul Too!*

How many times have you heard reports of dogs rescuing humans and other animals? It happens so often that the tendency is almost to take it for granted that a dog in your house serves as protection against intruders, an emergency alert system, and a fire alarm. Search-and-rescue dogs are welcome additions to police and fire departments, because they can dig people out from under rubble or find lost humans or pets. The year 2005 brought the earthquake and tsunami in the Indian Ocean, as well as news accounts of dogs carrying children to higher ground. In *Dogs That Know When Their Owners Are Coming Home*, the author and Harvard- and Cambridge-educated biochemist and philosopher

Rupert Sheldrake writes about a major earthquake that destroyed the Basilica of St. Francis of Assisi in Italy on September 26, 1997. "The night before, some dogs barked much more than usual; others were strangely agitated and restless."[1] Stories of animals exhibiting a "sixth sense" about an impending natural disaster have become accepted as odd, inexplicable, yet undeniably accurate. Too bad so few people know to pay attention to the dogs who are trying to warn them and save their lives.

But most dogs aren't heroes in the traditional sense of the word. Instead, they weave their heroics into people's lives so inextricably that it's often not until their relatively short lives are over that the family dog's natural bravery is recognized and remembered. That's why we have chosen stories for this chapter that wouldn't necessarily make headlines, although a couple of them could. We've decided to highlight quiet heroes, the courageous canines who bring and keep families together. The dogs who give of themselves every day to help seniors stay in their homes, with their remaining days full of joy and laughter. These are dogs who keep things going, who persist in ensuring that their human families will have a high quality of life. They are the dogs who teach children what it means to give without expecting a return.

When Linda was invited to a middle school to talk about what it's like to be an author, she asked if the children had pets and wanted to share a story about an animal who was special to them. One eleven-year-old boy raised his hand. He said that he, his dad, and his dog went ice fishing one Minnesota winter day. When his dad walked over to get something from the ice shack that they had placed on the lake, a patch of ice on which the boy was standing cracked and sent the child tumbling into the frigid water. The dog grabbed the boy's jacket and pulled him out of the water before the father could even run back to help.

As the boy told his story, the other children's eyes widened. They were obviously impressed at this astonishing rescue. Later, we couldn't help but wonder about hearing this story, a story the boy clearly hadn't even told his teacher or classmates. How many of these experiences with heroic dogs occur every day, all over the world, without ever having the dog's praises sung outside of the family circle?

We also hear everyday hero stories when we do radio interviews. People call in to tell about their own angel dogs. One man said that he works the night shift and comes home to sleep. But often he remains on call. When his cell phone rings, he must get up and take care of whatever situation has occurred. If he fails to answer a call, he could lose his job. One morning, the man went to sleep in his bedroom upstairs and forgot to put the cell phone on the nightstand near his bed. He had accidentally left it on a table downstairs. Still, he hadn't missed an important call: his dog, upon hearing the cell phone ring, grabbed the phone in his mouth, ran upstairs with it, and hurled the phone on top of the sleeping man. The phone was still ringing when the man woke up and answered it. Sure enough, he had to report back to work immediately.

No one would alert the media about this dog's problem-solving skills and the way he rescued his human from the unemployment line. But we think you'll enjoy reading the stories in this chapter about everyday champions. We certainly did. You're about to meet some outstanding dogs that give new definition to the word *hero*.

Make the acquaintance of:

- Tequila, a dog whose unique matchmaking ability sparks a romance between a man and a woman, and whose remarkable act of courage saves their family
- Poni, a dog who struggles to keep a man from being struck by a venomous snake
- A puppy who mysteriously appeared, came to an Ojibwe toddler's rescue, and disappeared just as mysteriously
- Gracie, a usually quiet and friendly dog who goes totally out of character with barking and agitation until her emergency message is understood
- Bonnie, a lovely golden retriever who transforms the life of an elderly couple with her constant devotion and service
- And of course Taylor, who reveals why dogs choose to be heroes.

As you reflect on the stories in this chapter, we hope you will remember the ordinary heroes who have rescued you in ways that may not be dramatic but certainly were effective and memorable.

Tequila, the Matchmaker Dog
Who Saved a Family

Caroline Kane Aquiar
San Ysidro, California

When I was only nineteen years old, I became the manager of my own business — boarding stables on the outskirts of the San Fernando Valley in the City of Angels, Los Angeles. My friends, co-owners of the property, helped me to start the business. One of our first transactions was to rent a small trailer on the property to a young man who had recently moved to the area. My friends, who rented him the trailer, had met the man. But since he worked all day and well into the night, and I worked days, I hadn't seen him yet.

My mornings at the stables began bright and early. I was usually there by seven o'clock, ready to begin feeding the horses and cleaning the stalls of my nine horse boarders. One morning I parked my car in its usual spot, which happened to be near the new tenant's trailer. I noticed a large new doghouse outside it. A small black-and-white dog sat inside. I guessed by his long hair and coloring that the dog was a young border collie. I called to him, and he came to me, happily wagging his tail so hard that his whole body shook with excitement. Because the dog was attached to the house by a long chain, it seemed obvious that our renter didn't want the dog running off while he was away at work.

With all the work I had to do, the days flew by. This dog and I became fast friends, especially when I began bringing dog biscuits for him every day. I never saw the young man, but his dog looked well fed and cared for. He sure was an energetic little character and wanted to play all the time.

One day I decided to untie the dog. I hoped that he knew and trusted me well enough to stay nearby. I had a lot of chores to do and figured that the lonely dog and I could keep each other company while I worked. The second I untied him, the dog started running circles around me, playfully jumping and dodging. From that moment on, he always accompanied me on my rounds at the stables. Of course, during all this play and good cheer, I forgot that my new friend really belonged to someone else. One day I was outside, stacking hay bales for the horses. The dog lay in the sun beside me as I worked. I noticed a blue Volkswagen van pull up next to the trailer. Minutes later, I heard a voice calling, "Tequila! Tequila!" followed by whistling.

The dog quickly sat up and cocked his head to one side. I waited to see what he would do. Surely the young man was wondering where his dog had gone and would come looking for him. I had grown so used to this dog's company that it hadn't even occurred to me, till that moment, that I had done something wrong by untying him without permission. Upon realizing this, my heart skipped a beat. I nervously looked in the direction of the whistles and saw the young man walking toward us. As he approached, the dog wagged his tail excitedly but did not run to him.

"Tequila?" the man called softly.

Tequila answered with vigorous tail wagging.

I smiled, not knowing what to say. I blurted out the first thing that came to mind. "Oh, is that his name?" I asked.

Looking at his dog, the man said, "Looks like you've found another buddy, haven't you, boy?" He patted Tequila on the head.

I put down my baling hooks and walked over to the man. "You know, I'm really sorry about this. I shouldn't have untied your dog. He seemed so friendly and eager to play. I always tie him up again before I leave and check to make sure he has plenty of water. I hope you don't mind."

The young man fell silent. I felt like a fool but continued anyway. "Did you know he likes doggy biscuits?" I asked cheerfully.

Without looking at me, the man replied, "Yes, I did. I found a pile of them in my closet. I guess he's

Caroline and Raul's Tequila with Ricky

saving them for something." He glanced my way with a teasing look in his eyes, and we both burst out laughing!

Tequila must have known something good was unfolding, because he joined in on our laughter with loud barks. The young man introduced himself to me as Raul. From that day forward, we became friends. Raul started driving home like a madman after work, trying to get back to the stables before I left for the day. He began helping me with the horses.

About a month after Tequila brought us together, I arrived at the stables early one morning to discover that all of the corrals were perfectly clean. The horses had been fed. And inside each of the feed bins, Raul had placed a red rose. That was the day he asked me to go out with him for an official dinner date. This time, Tequila wasn't invited to join us.

I remember how nervous I felt on our first date. To make things worse, Raul ran out of gas on the freeway at ten o'clock that night. He was so embarrassed.

We were never party people or big on socializing, so the story of our courtship isn't exciting. All I can say is that somehow I knew Raul was the guy I wanted to spend the rest of my life with. One year after we met, we were married and became a family with Tequila. We just celebrated our eighteenth wedding anniversary this year.

From the first time I saw him, I sensed that Tequila was a very special dog. The only thing he lacked was the ability to speak. Raul and I even wondered about *that*, because the expressions Tequila got on his face and in his eyes spoke to us loud and clear. The old saying is that the eyes are windows to the soul. Tequila's eyes pulled Raul and me through those windows and opened the doors to our own souls, filling us with insight and inspiration. Of course, because Tequila had been our matchmaker, Raul and I felt a very special connection with this dog. I think Tequila felt the same way about us. He was our constant friend during the early years of married life.

Then our son Ricky was born. On Ricky's first night home from the hospital, Tequila, in his own way, sent us another clear message: his job was to protect the new baby. I remember the first time I put my son in his new crib. Tequila walked over and sniffed everything that held the baby's scent. He then laid down next to the crib and didn't move for the rest of the night. This continued every night. When Ricky cried, I was also awakened by Tequila nudging me with his cold nose. It was as if he were saying, "Hey, come on, get up. The baby needs you."

Raul, Ricky, Tequila, and I lived across the street from a beautiful park. As my son grew older, I began taking him in the afternoons to the park for fresh air and sunshine. Of course, Tequila accompanied us. He loved to run around and visit with other neighborhood dogs while I chatted with their human companions. Naturally, people would stop and ask about the baby. Interestingly enough, when someone cooed over Ricky, Tequila sat very close to the stroller and watched everything. My son's guardian was always on the job!

One unfortunate day, we were out in front of our house and another dog was in the park. Tequila saw him and shot out across the street, just as a car was coming. The car hit him, and his left hind leg was broken in two places. It required surgery and two aluminum plates. After the accident, Tequila needed constant attention. We took care of him without question. My husband woke up two or three times each night to give Tequila medication and carry him outside to urinate. Our dog did recover eventually, but he was never the same again. Because of joint stiffness and physical limitations, he began gaining weight, and he developed arthritis in his bad leg. Winter, with its colder weather, became a terrible time for him.

Months later we bought our first house and were settling in quite nicely. My son was now six months old and tearing through the house in his walker. Boy, did he know how to maneuver that walker around corners and down hallways. I could barely keep up with him! During beautiful summer days, I always kept the front door open but shut the screen door with the latch tightly in place. Directly outside our front door was a porch with three concrete steps, about five feet wide, leading down from it. There was a three-foot drop-off from the steps into the bushes below.

One afternoon, while Raul was at work, I was washing dishes in the kitchen. I could hear Ricky running his walker on the living room floor. As long as I heard movement and Ricky's happy squeals, I knew that he was all right. But when the screen door opened, I dropped everything and raced to the front door. I found Ricky braced against Tequila's body. The baby's walker was dangerously tilted at a forty-five-degree angle, hovering over the edge of the steps. Apparently, Tequila had heard Ricky flying out the door. He had positioned his body in front of Ricky, miraculously preventing what could have been a very serious injury to our son.

At the same moment that I found Ricky and Tequila, my husband pulled into our driveway. Raul and I froze in our tracks, unable to believe what was happening. The arthritic Tequila continued to stand firmly against the baby's body, while Ricky playfully pulled the dog's fluffy hair and patted his back. Finally, Tequila looked at us as if to say, "Well, aren't you going to come and get him?" We hurried over and grabbed the baby.

Neither my husband nor I will ever forget how Tequila saved my son from having a potentially fatal accident. Tequila was always a wonderful friend, and I do believe that he became my son's guardian angel during those baby and toddler years. He brought so much joy and love into all of our lives. As Ricky grew, he and Tequila spent a lot of time together. From an early age, Tequila showed Ricky about love and friendship with animals. This is something special that Ricky still carries in his heart today at the age of sixteen.

Tequila was truly our angel — the dog who brought my husband and me together and saved our son's young life. We will always be grateful for his love.

Meditation

Has a dog ever served as a matchmaker for you? Have you found dogs to be excellent judges of character?

Poni Faces a Poisonous Rattlesnake

Del Langheld
Minden, Louisiana

*W*e got Poni when she was an eight-month-old puppy. My son, Chris, brought her home in his arms one night after visiting a friend in town. The people Poni had belonged to didn't want her anymore and were going to dump her somewhere. So I knew this puppy really needed a home.

She was scared and weak and needed a bath desperately. It took almost a week for her to get used to us, but she grew to be a beautiful mixed-breed white dog with black and brown spots. Our family got a chuckle out of the funny way Poni had of listening with her ears standing straight up.

When the weather was warm, Poni always wanted to be outside in our yard. She played there during the day but came inside the house at night. One day, we had to go to town to buy groceries. As we were coming up our driveway, we saw Poni, standing frozen and still, with every hair on her body sticking straight out. She looked like her hair had been dried in the dryer.

As we came closer, we could see Poni growling and showing her teeth. I told my husband, Tommy, that something had to be wrong with the dog. When he opened the car door, Poni growled even louder.

Tommy got out of the car. Poni turned her eyes toward him and growled so loud that it sounded like a freight train. Every hair on her body stretched out as far as it could.

At first we couldn't see anything that would make the dog so upset. When Tommy moved closer to Poni, he finally saw why she was growling. It was her way of warning us away. On the ground in front of her, a baby rattlesnake was coiled up, ready to strike.

Tommy came as near to the snake as he dared, and Poni barked again. The snake struck and bit her right on the lip. Poni slumped to the ground as my husband removed the snake. I watched in horror as Poni's lip began to swell. I was afraid she would die right then.

We ran into the house with Poni. I called the vet, who said that Poni would probably be all right. He did not have any antivenin, and even if he ordered it, he said, it would take at least three days to arrive. He told me to keep an eye on the dog and call if she got worse.

We made Poni as comfortable as possible. She refused to eat or drink water. I prayed and asked the Lord to let this courageous dog live. I knew we would continue to give her a good life.

Poni's lip swelled as big as a baseball. Then, after three or four days, the swelling finally went down, and she seemed to be back to nor-

Del's Poni

mal. She started jumping around, wanting to go outside, and eating again. We kept her inside until she was feeling 100 percent better. But

75

that snakebite left a big white scar on the top of her lip and the bottom of her black nose.

We will never forget how Poni risked her life to save Tommy and me from being bit by the baby rattlesnake. I couldn't see the snake, because it blended in with the dirt and rocks in the driveway. Poni would not let us get close enough to see what was upsetting her. It was amazing how Poni protected us. We believe that we owe our lives to this dog. She knew that this seven-inch snake was dangerous. I have always heard that a baby rattlesnake is more deadly, and the venom is more powerful than that from a full-grown snake. I don't know what a snakebite like that would do to a human. But I am grateful that Poni barked so that the snake struck her and not Tommy. She will always be our guardian.

Meditation

When has a dog acted out of character to warn you that something was amiss or dangerous?

The Puppy Who Belonged to No One

Jeanne Croud
Minneapolis, Minnesota

*M*y family is Native American, of the Minnesota Ojibwe tribe. I wanted my fifteen-month-old daughter to be given her Indian name by a woman, so I made arrangements to take her to a *namer*, an Ojibwe female elder I admired. The woman's husband is also a spiritual elder, from a related tribe. The couple were so charmed by my daughter that they asked if each of them could give her a name. They invited my family to attend a semiannual feast that their family traditionally gives each spring and fall to honor the eagles. At that time, they also planned to give names to several people.

We traveled to the land the couple owned in a remote area of northern Wisconsin. The setting was beautiful. There were log buildings, a sweat lodge, and an enormous permanent teepee where the ceremonies are held. Down a fairly steep hill was the edge of a wonderful but very deep lake. Lots of kids and dogs roamed and played in the area. I noticed among them a particularly nondescript half-grown brown puppy who didn't seem to belong to anyone.

On the morning of the naming ceremony, I was in one of the buildings, helping to make food for the feast. I had left my daughter with her father looking after her. As I peeled potatoes, I suddenly became edgy and very concerned for my daughter. The woman who was going to give my daughter her name looked at me several times and asked what was wrong. I told her I thought I should check on my daughter. She said, "Go immediately. A mother's first responsibility is to her children."

I raced outside, where I found my husband concentrating on helping someone fix a car. As quick toddlers will do, my daughter had wandered away from him and was heading determinedly for the lake. She must have started walking toward the deep water as soon as her dad had turned his back. I swooped her up into my arms and took her away from the lake.

After that, I turned to speak with the children who were playing nearby. They told me that my daughter couldn't make it to the lake, because the small brown puppy I had seen earlier had constantly herded her away from the water, as a sheepdog would. The children, who played nearby, said that the puppy had blocked each of my daughter's attempts to get to the lake. Grateful to the puppy, I returned with my little girl to the building, where I went back to helping prepare the meal.

Later that day, in the traditional ceremony, my daughter received her Indian name. Many of our elders teach us that the name we're given is the name of the spirit who watches over us. The woman and her husband had each planned to give my daughter a separate name, but it turned out that they were both guided to the same name for her. My daughter's Indian name from that day on became *Anjeni Equay*. In English it means *Angel Woman*.

As far as I can tell, no one ever again saw the puppy who belonged to no one. The puppy disappeared after staying long enough to save my little Angel Woman's life.

Meditation

Could there have been dogs who quickly came into and went out of your life but stayed long enough to perform an important service?

Gracie, Our Hostess Dog

Pam Thorsen
Hastings, Minnesota

*W*e own two bed-and-breakfast inns that were built in 1880. I am not sure if our lovely auburn-and-white springer, Gracie, just came by it naturally, or if we somehow trained her to understand that our guests were her guests, but Gracie was a hostess who lived up to her name. She never barked at guests, always greeting them with a tail wag and the kindest intentions. She would drop her green tennis ball by their feet, but she never pushed it at them. She only sighed as if to say, "You may throw the ball for me if you like, but if not, that's fine. I will simply be here, if you need entertainment. I am here to serve the guests."

Gracie lived with us in the servants' quarters and knew she was not allowed in the inn part of the house. We are respectful of guests who may have allergies. And we certainly did not want any guests to say something negative to our dear dog. But Gracie had full run of the fenced backyard, which included the guests' porch. Sometimes, when we served dinner or breakfast to the guests in the dining room, Gracie would wait for them to come outside and relax on the porch. She entertained them with a game of fetch or simply rested on the porch rug within petting range of the swing and the rocking chair.

One evening, after we had served dinner to a couple of guests who especially liked dogs, I let Gracie outside from our kitchen to take a romp in the yard. I cannot see the dining room from the kitchen, but I could see the yard and heard Gracie barking incessantly. I watched her barking in the direction of the porch, where the guests might have been enjoying the swing. I thought it was rude for Gracie to carry on as if she were quite angry. By then, her barking had escalated into growling, and she barked louder and louder. I yelled, "Gracie, come in here right now. Quit that. Shame on you." She continued barking frantically, looking at me and then running toward the porch, and barking even more insistently.

I felt embarrassed. I had bragged to this couple about what a kind, loving dog Gracie always is. They were looking forward to meeting her and said that they absolutely adored springers. I realized that I would have to go out to the yard and bring Gracie inside. She was not giving up, even though I had scolded her for barking. When I walked out into the yard, I looked toward the house. I assumed that I'd see my guests sitting on the porch, frustrated or annoyed by this strange behavior of our loving Gracie. Instead, the porch was empty, and my guests were nowhere in sight. I looked

Pam's Gracie

toward the dining room. That's when I realized what had upset Gracie. Through the window, I saw four-foot-tall flames shooting up within the dining room.

As Gracie continued to bark, I ran into the house. Gracie followed me, barking all the way. When we arrived in the dining room, I was horrified. The guests must have finished dinner and retired for the evening, leaving the candles lit. The glass candleholder had cracked, and the candle had spilled onto the tablecloth and ignited it. I quickly smothered the flames with the doubled-over cloth and poured a pitcher of water from the side table to extinguish the fire.

Gracie stayed right by my side this whole time. She wasn't about to leave me alone to handle this problem. Our alert dog had warned me about the fire before the alarms and sprinklers went off. She had saved the day! I gave her the biggest hugs and asked for forgiveness. I should have known our grace-filled wonder dog was barking with good reason. For our darling hostess Gracie's hospitality always filled our home and inn with joy.

Meditation

Who are the Gracies in your life? What dogs (or people) are good at letting you know when your emotional fires are burning out of control?

Bonnie, Our Everyday Hero

Richard and Marjorie Douse
St. Paul, Minnesota

*L*ife in our home without a dog was way too quiet. No joyous greetings at the door. Because laughter is ever-present with a dog in the home, and six-dozen laughs throughout the day are normal, we found ourselves missing precious communication with someone other than a human.

With previous pets, we had always loved how our dogs made eye contact and exchanged silent understanding with us. And it was helpful when one of us dropped a food item while we were cooking: a dog would immediately pick it up, which meant that neither of us had to bend down. At our ages, bending can be quite a pain! A dog companion offered a kind of understanding that is different from human understanding. Dogs could read our moods and feelings quicker than people did. We missed having those qualities in our lives.

After observing older people with small dogs, we realized it would be easier for us to have a large dog, who would not require that we bend down in order to pet and care for her. We had wanted a golden retriever for many years, and finally, right after we both retired, we got Bonnie, our first golden puppy. We highly recommend this breed for its even, loving temperament. Bonnie turned

83

out to be the healthiest dog we ever had. She rarely had to see her doctor, except for yearly exams and inoculations.

Bonnie soon became an indispensable member of our family. She brought in the newspaper and the mail and carried up and down the stairs, in her mouth, notes that we wrote to each other. This meant that we didn't have to make so many trips between the floors of our multilevel home. We never felt alone when Bonnie was in the house. As we aged and tended to go out less, she provided us with loving companionship.

Richard and Marjorie's Bonnie

In retirement we found ourselves able to enjoy more time with our canine family member than we had with previous pets, sometimes playing, other times just petting and looking into her eyes. Each morning, when Richard barely had moved an eyelid, Bonnie would position herself alongside the bed to enjoy having her whole body massaged, which usually lasted twenty to thirty minutes. This is something neither of us ever wanted to miss, and it became a wonderful way to begin the day. The last thing we did at night, when preparing for bed, was brushing Bonnie's teeth, which became another ritual we all enjoyed.

Being older "parents," we had to consider what would become of Bonnie if something were to happen to one or both of us. We decided to provide for the dog in our wills. We consulted with our daughter and son-in-law, who would take excellent care of her. We felt comforted to know that they would be delighted to take over Bonnie's care and offer her the same spiritual exchange between animal and human that she had always known with us.

Our quality of life was definitely enhanced by Bonnie's presence. When she was eight weeks old, we started taking her on visits to a retirement and nursing home complex to visit our older relatives. Those visits often became quite lengthy when residents and staff asked to pet the dog as we walked through the halls. Bonnie would romp right up to the entrance of the nursing home, but settled down as she walked inside. She never jumped up or acted rowdy while greeting the elderly residents. It was obvious she cherished these experiences. And she brought so much joy to everyone she met.

When Richard's aunt Alice suffered a broken hip at age ninety-eight and was failing fast, we took Bonnie to see her. Bonnie went close to the head of the dying woman's bed and placed her head near auntie's. Then Bonnie cried, whimpering, as we had never heard her do before. Aunt Alice died a few days later.

After we'd had Bonnie for about eight years, Marjorie experienced an emotional crisis with her older sister, which left her feeling depressed. We believe that Marjorie's depression was obvious to Bonnie before Marjorie even realized her condition. Marjorie's life slowed down a lot. She went out only when necessary and didn't drive for a couple of months. She found herself gravitating to the brightest room in the house, her little sewing room with windows on three sides. She took up quilting in earnest, and Bonnie stayed with her constantly. Bonnie would even abandon her game of fetch with Richard when Marjorie went to the sewing room. This became Marjorie's very touching, loving time with our dog.

After staying near Marjorie for a while, Bonnie would run downstairs to go outside. Then she would arrive back in the sewing room with a note from Richard to Marjorie, saying our lunch was ready in the kitchen. Bonnie seemed to know that she played an important role in helping Marjorie to heal, which she did, eventually. Marjorie believes that Bonnie's role in her recovery was as important as the help she received from Richard, her doctor, her pastor, and her family.

When she was nine and a half years old, Bonnie's death came as a complete surprise. On the day that she died, Bonnie ate well. The night before, she had run up and down the stairs, full of her usual pep and energy. When we awoke the morning of her last day, we found her panting noisily and realized she must be seriously ill. We had to arrange for a neighbor to help carry Bonnie downstairs and to the car so we could take her for medical help.

While Richard was phoning for the neighbor to come over, Marjorie laid her head on Bonnie's and put her hand on the dog's body. She could hear Bonnie's breathing becoming shallower. When Richard returned to the room, Bonnie lifted her head to look at him, wagged her tail twice, and then there was no further sign of life.

We took Bonnie to the vet. She came out to the car to examine Bonnie and confirmed that our beloved dog was gone. We both collapsed against the car and sobbed. Such a beautiful part of our lives had disappeared in only half an hour. It was impossible to believe. We felt that it had been such a blessing that as her last act on earth, Bonnie had shown her love for us: twelve days before Bonnie died, Marjorie had begun tapering off the antidepressant she had been taking. It was as if this loving dog had waited to leave until she knew her "mommy" would be all right. Our only consolation with Bonnie's sudden death was the gratitude we felt that she had not suffered for long.

Our home was unbelievably empty after Bonnie died. We had so loved this beautiful creature bouncing around and making our home full of life for so many years. Two days later, at five in the afternoon, we could no longer stand the emptiness and grief. We left for a five-day trip to Door County, Wisconsin. At every stop along the way, it seemed that angels were sent in the form of dog lovers to comfort us.

Our family doctor had always reminded us how important it is for older people to have a pet. On our visits to his office, he would ask how the dog was, remembering the many times we had told him of the important improvements Bonnie made in our lives. After Bonnie died, we asked the doctor if he thought we should adopt another dog at our ages of seventy-five and eighty. He told us that we should never be without a dog.

Although, of course, no dog can ever replace Bonnie, we are happy to say that we now have another golden retriever puppy in our family. When people ask why we seem so young for our ages, we credit our dogs.

Bonnie was a precious gift from God, bringing us much joy and deeper understanding of God's creation.

Meditation

Has Bonnie's story helped you to rethink whether you're too old to adopt and raise a dog? What purpose would be served by having a dog in your life at any stage?

Ask Taylor

Dear Taylor,

Why is it that dogs are so quick to save people's lives and don't hesitate to do brave deeds?

Sincerely,
Timid

Dear Timid,

A long time ago, dogs were given the gift of unconditional love. This meant that they have hearts as big as mountains. Because we dogs love as God loves, unconditionally, our first thoughts are to help and serve anyone who needs us.

Courage carries our love into the world on golden paws. Saving others and making their days brighter are as natural to us as breathing.

Heroically yours,

Taylor

What book about dogs would be complete without acknowledging how much fun they are? The next chapter takes you into the playful, creative, and never dull world of doggy comedians and joyful companions.

CHAPTER THREE

Can You Catch Joyrides on Wagging Tails?

I'm a poor underdog,
But tonight I will bark
With the great Overdog
That romps through the dark.

— Robert Frost, "Canis Major"

We have always joked that if animals bought books, ours would never be off the bestseller lists. Dogs would paw through the books, wagging their tails and reading stories to each other before they dozed off to sleep at night. Cats would cuddle up with one of our books, twitching their whiskers with pleasure and purring from cover to cover. Birds would deposit feathers between the pages as bookmarks. Bookworms would...well, you get the picture.

You can imagine our surprise and amusement when dogs really did let us know that they had found joy in our books. Following are a few stories, with a couple of photos included (see pages 12 and 93) to let you in on the fun.

Picture this:

We're at a nursing home where the residents aren't all convinced that it's a good idea to have pets there. After we do our presentation, read some stories, and ask the staff to tell us about the dogs and cats who have alerted them to patients in danger, the mood changes to one of more acceptance and appreciation. As an expression of gratitude, the two resident dogs in the facility, who have been sitting in the back of the room listening, rush up after we finish speaking. They jump up and down, lick our cheeks, and offer their silent thank-yous for telling these people about how well and how often they have kept the residents healthy or saved their lives.

Picture this:

We are working night and day to finish the manuscript for our first book, about the spiritual connection between people and animals. We decide to take a break and go for a walk. When we step outside our door, two beautiful collies tear away from their human companion, run over to us, and vigorously lick our hands, their tails wagging joyously. The woman who is walking the dogs is embarrassed. She calls to them, but they won't return until they have finished expressing appreciation, we assume, for the stories we're writing that will help people understand animals better. The woman apologizes. "They have never run off from me before," she says. "I don't know what happened." We do.

Picture this:

In a bookstore that shall remain nameless, there has been a mix-up.

In spite of our publicist's best efforts, the store manager doesn't seem to realize that we're supposed to be having a presentation for our book *God's Messengers: What Animals Teach Us about the Divine*. He's only set up a table for a signing. We know of at least thirty people who are coming, including contributing authors from that city. They are all expecting a workshop at which they will show photos of their pets and share their stories in a lovefest for animals.

After we help the manager set up chairs and clear a space for the event, we begin the presentation. When two of the attendees show up at the bookstore with their dogs, the manager allows them inside. (Out of guilt, maybe?) The dogs sit quietly, listening intently to the presentation. After it is over, Gail and Rich Roeske's dog, Annie, tears away from Gail, jumps up on the table where we are autographing books, and plants a big, wet, sloppy kiss on Linda's mouth. Another dog can't resist sitting on Linda's lap while she signs books.

Gail and Rich Roeske's Annie kisses Linda

Guess we were right: animals really do love our books!

These experiences are only a few of the many times when dogs have made us laugh and brightened our lives with their warmth, exuberance, and charm. You certainly have your own stories, if you've ever lived with a dog. And you probably gravitate toward others who understand what dogs are all about. We were amused but not surprised to see that there are websites that make romantic matches between dog lovers.

Before we move forward in this chapter, with its delightful stories about dogs as funny friends and cuddly comedians, we want to share a piece from that Internet jokester "Unknown." You know, the one who passes jokes around the World Wide Web that break up your day with a bit of laughter.

If Dogs Were Our Teachers

If dogs were our teachers, we would learn important stuff like:

- When loved ones come home, always run to greet them like they've been gone for a year.

- Never pass up the opportunity to go for a joyride in the car.

- Allow the experience of fresh air and the wind in your face to be pure ecstasy.

- Take naps.

- Run, romp, and play daily.

- Thrive on attention and let people touch you.

- On warm days, stop to lie on your back on the grass.

- Delight in the simple joy of taking a long walk.

- Eat with gusto and enthusiasm.

- When someone is having a bad day, be silent, sit close by, and nuzzle them.

- When you're happy, dance around and wiggle your entire body.

Join us now in this chapter, where you'll meet the following doggy masters of relaxation and fun:

- Pinkey, a dog who became adept at stealing balls from a nearby fairground and preserving letters from her wartime buddy

- Adam, a golden Lab who befriended two faithful swans for a long-term relationship at a country lake

- Booger, a rambunctious puppy who specializes in high-spirited destruction, joyful escape from the yard, and compassionate friendship

- Presty, a springer-sheltie mix who discovered a clever and creative way to express her joy without all the noise and commotion

- Sierra, an exuberant dog who taught her human how to live in the moment

- Gambit, the dog who taught a fifty-something woman how to handle middle age gracefully and cheerfully, and Tycho, their aged canine friend, who is teaching them both how to live well in their senior years

- Fi-Fi, Susie, and Charlie, who inspired a family to hold an annual Dog Day to celebrate the human-dog relationships that bring year-round joy

· Taylor, who taught the Andersons a lesson or two about balance and the importance of playing, and who goes on, in "Ask Taylor," to enlighten us all on the canine sense of humor.

Put your feet up, sip your favorite beverage, and get into a playful mood. Dogs are going to show you how your life can be much more fun.

Pinkey

Bob Shaw
Benton, Missouri

$\mathcal{S}$eems like I was around nine years old when she came to live with us. For quite some time, Dad had wanted a blond cocker spaniel. One day, friends of my parents had a litter of puppies to sell, and one of the dogs was a blond cocker. In those days, the price they were asking, twenty-five dollars, was quite a sum to pay for a puppy. Mom was pretty firm with her no.

After a while, Dad talked Mom into taking a trip to see the litter. It only took one look at a little blond with just a tint of red and a nose full of freckles to change her mind. In no time at all, Pinkey became our family dog.

There was very little in her new home that Pinkey didn't consider to be hers, including me, her only kid. It also wasn't long before she regarded as her property shoes, furniture, and anything else chewable. One of her favorite tricks was to shine our shoes. She'd roll over on her back, wiggling and squirming on top of our shoes until she thought they were shined. The more we laughed, the harder she'd work at it.

Pinkey was fascinated by living next to the fairground. She burrowed a hole under the fence and crawled through it to take whatever adventure happened to come her way. At the fairground, near the hole Pinkey had dug from our yard, a booth was set up where people played the game of throwing a baseball at milk bottles. Pinkey, who loved to play fetch, would sneak under the tent and grab the ball when it hit the ground. Then she'd head for the hole under our fence with her long ears flapping in the breeze, carrying the ball in her mouth.

Before we knew it, baseballs filled our yard. Dad worried that Pinkey might be caught and punished for her thievery. He gathered up as many of the balls as he could find and took them back to the fairground to return them to the game's owner. Dad explained what was happening and said that he wanted to make sure Pinkey wouldn't be hurt. Dad promised that he'd bring back all the balls Pinkey stole.

Bob's Pinkey

The man started laughing. He told Dad that everyone had been watching Pinkey steal the balls. They all thought it was the cutest thing they'd ever seen. The man assured Dad that no one would hurt our little dog, but he would appreciate having the baseballs returned regularly.

Over the next several years, we'd occasionally find an old baseball in some hidden spot in the yard. Its discovery would always bring back memories of Pinkey's robberies.

I graduated from high school and enlisted in the U.S. Air Force. Whenever I came home on leave, Pinkey would always be the last one I said good-bye to. She seemed to understand every word I ever said to her. Those big brown eyes held so much intelligence. Then I was sent to Vietnam, on the other side of the world from Pinkey and the rest of my family.

Pinkey met my first letter that arrived home from Vietnam with a lot of barking and enthusiasm. She had caught my scent on the letter. When my family had finished reading it, they left the letter on the kitchen table. Pinkey sneaked up onto the chair and snatched the letter. Later, Mom found Pinkey curled up in her bed with my letter tucked under her chin. "You little thief," she said. Then Pinkey gazed at Mom with watery eyes, pointed to the letter with her nose, and looked back at her. "It just broke my heart," Mom said.

From then on, Pinkey ended up with all my letters. She kept them on her bed and slept with them every night.

Several years later, Mom called my home to tell me that Pinkey had passed on. She had lived to be almost sixteen years old. Mom and Dad put Pinkey to rest in the backyard that she had loved so much. I found a marble slab to carve her name into, to serve as her tombstone. Thirty years later, I can still walk out to the backyard and see it, just as it was back then, after Pinkey left us.

A few years ago, Dad had some work done under the house. The workman came out with what was left of an old baseball. We all smiled and said, "The little thief!"

There's a place called the Rainbow Bridge, where animals and their human companions are reunited in the afterlife. There, a little blond cocker spaniel with a freckled nose snatches dropped baseballs and plays with them while she waits for us to join her someday.

Meditation

How many "little thieves" of your heart have you known? When has a dog shown you that he or she misses you more than words could express?

Incident at Lake Isabella

Kathy Broderick
Chicago, Illinois

*Y*ears ago, my husband and I purchased a small Chicago bungalow with a tiny backyard. We promptly began to fill up our home. First came the puppy: Adam, a golden Lab with huge paws. Those were carefree puppy days — Adam sliding along the hardwood floors across the length of the empty house, dog Frisbee in the park, trips to the dog beach. Then came the children: twin girls, with twice the usual amount of baby gear. As my husband and I took on the responsibilities of parenthood, Adam accepted this situation and grew into a loyal, protective member of the family.

Everyone needs to get out of the city on occasion, especially a ninety-pound Lab like Adam. Lucky for all of us, my parents own a cottage on Lake Isabella, a small lake without beaches. The surrounding forest thins naturally as it meets the water, and the homes are set back from the shore, up a slight incline, and not easily visible from the water. Lake Isabella is not a lake for water-skiers. It's a fishing lake. Paddleboats, canoes, and the occasional small motorized fishing boat scoot by. Children float around on rafts, sometimes even reaching the opposite shore. And two swans made their home there.

Regardless of the time of day or year, as soon as our family turned onto the two-lane highway in our old Jeep and neared Lake Isabella, Adam popped his head up over the backseat. When we hit the dirt road, his tail began to wag. The closer we got to the lake and cabin, the harder he wagged his tail and refused to sit down. Upon arrival, we opened the hatch, and Adam bolted straight for the water. Then he ran back up the hill to us, wildly. Up and down the hill, in and out of the water, he frolicked joyfully, off his leash all weekend long.

From the porch of my parents' cottage, the grand view of the lake is the thing — like a giant movie screen displaying nature. And the swans were often the movie stars. They swam so regally across the lake, like a royal procession.

Kathy's Adam

I remember the day when the swans and Adam first met. My mom, my sister, and I were sitting on the porch, curiously watching two alien species about to encounter each other for the first time. Adam was swimming, with just his head visible, and a wake trailing behind him. The swans and the dog approached each other at the same speed. Those swan bodies looked so huge, even from far away. Adam was a big dog, but since his bulk was invisible and kind of useless under water, it seemed like he was at a disadvantage.

Adam kept approaching the swans. I ran down the hill and called to him from the shore. He wouldn't listen. He was way out in

102

the lake and deep into the swans' territory. They leaned down and hissed at him. Adam was not a stupid dog. He quickly turned around and hustled back to shore. Having dismissed him, the swans turned to leave. But Adam stood on the shore, wagging his tail and tracking them with his eyes.

Again and again, the swans and Adam approached each other in the lake, and at some point during that weekend, they became playmates. Their first meeting had been funny and frightening. Their eventual friendship became warm and reliable. They clearly came to understand each other.

Whenever we arrived at the lake, our dog ran down to the shore. Within moments, the swans swam over to greet him. With a kind of dog radar, he called out to them, and with some dog sense, he knew they would come. I was always surprised that they did. I never knew anyone so dependable as those swans coming back to Adam. It was something to aspire to.

Then Adam got sick. He filled up with sorrow. One day, when the four of us went out on the boat, he sat at the shoreline and howled like a wolf. We had never heard such a sound from his mouth. The lake seemed to have taught him how to express himself, and what he wanted to say was that he could not bear to be alone. We rushed back to him, frightened. Within the month, we were explaining to our four-year-old daughters that Adam had gone to Doggy Heaven.

We couldn't bury Adam in our backyard at home. He was too big, and our yard was so small. And besides, it just didn't seem right. We kept his ashes in a box for weeks before we realized what we needed to do.

One beautiful October day, my husband, our daughters, and I took Adam's ashes to Lake Isabella. We looked around and agreed that a forested spot by the shore would be the best burial site. While walking down the hill, we said a prayer to St. Francis, the patron saint of animals, and then started scattering Adam's ashes in this perfect spot. We said our tearful good-byes to him.

And then, a flash of white, two flashes of light. Swimming out from the cover of the forest, from around the bend, the swans approached our private ceremony. Instead of parading across the lake, they had sneaked in the back door like celebrities avoiding the paparazzi. They came looking for their friend, to say good-bye. They stayed for only a minute, as if to give their blessings, then left the way they came. In retrospect, I believe that this was the last time I ever saw the swans on Lake Isabella.

My dog is gone now. And so are the swans. But it's easy for me to visualize their dance. It was natural and beautiful and mysterious and funny. It was something I never saw in the city: animals unleashed and unfenced, animals minus their humans, an animal utopia! Their simple, unchanging relationship effortlessly spanned three full years. As humans, we watched them, amazed and mystified.

Adam is not filled with sorrow anymore. And he's not alone. I know that, because the swans came to tell me so. When they appeared at Adam's funeral, it was as if to tell me that Adam had joined all animals who die an honorable death. Their brief appearance assured me that Adam's suffering had ended, and that all he would feel now was the natural rhythm of the changing seasons.

At Adam's funeral, I learned that he wasn't a city dog. A dog belongs to a family, but a dog belongs to a place as well. Doggy Heaven is that place. And for Adam, Doggy Heaven is a place called Lake Isabella.

Meditation

Are there people or animals who want to form unlikely friendships with you? Is there someone who is very different from you but could enrich your life in a unique way?

The Booger Dog

Pamela Jenkins
Henryetta, Oklahoma

We called him The Booger. I remember the spring morning when my family drove to a friend's home in the country to see their litter of purebred beagle puppies. We were hoping to adopt one into our family but were having a hard time deciding which puppy was the pick of the litter. Each one was bright-eyed and sweet and so huggable. Then my son saw one large puppy that didn't look anything at all like his brothers and sisters. He said, "Hey, look at that little booger over there!" My son insisted on taking home the oddball of the group. Try as I might to call the puppy a more noble name like Duke or King, the term Booger just seemed to fit him better.

Our new puppy looked like a short Saint Bernard with wiry hair and flyaway ears. From his first day in our home, he was all teeth and puddles, mischief and destruction. He could have been a poster puppy for obedience training gone wild. A rolled-up newspaper meant a fine game of catch-me-if-you-can. A scolding seemed to fall on deaf floppy ears. But with his bright eyes, flapping tongue, and wagging tail, he looked so funny that it was hard for me to stay mad at him. It never occurred to The Booger that he could be in trouble.

Soon his sharp, little puppy barks matured into deep, throaty bays. An autumn leaf blowing across the yard at night was reason enough for The Booger to sound the alarm and raise the family from our sleep. He dug holes in the garden with joyful abandon. He freely watered the begonias and geraniums. Anything left within his reach was buried, carried under the house, or devoured. The Booger welcomed door-to-door salesmen. He liked children and hated baths. He preferred his cats to be surprised and running. When I took The Booger on a country walk one day, I spent ten minutes enjoying the walk and the next two hours searching and calling for him.

The Booger became an accomplished escape artist, and keeping him at home was often a challenge. Using his nose, he would nuzzle the gate latch free when someone forgot to lock it. Once the gate was opened, he would race away to play with the

Pamela's sister Sandra with The Booger

neighborhood children. Our family would chase him down the street and around in circles, but The Booger didn't want to be caught. He was just having too much fun and would not come home until he was ready. At the end of the day, he would run up on our porch and flop down with a sigh, happy and tired. By that time, The Booger had become more a source of frustration than of fun.

One spring day, The Booger came home his usual way: by climbing over the honeysuckle vine that grew on the back fence. He dropped into the yard and interrupted the garden club meeting I was hosting on our patio. Tea glasses were lowered and eyebrows rose as our dog demonstrated to the ladies how to reach a certain itch by sitting down and scooting across the ground. My guests never forgot meeting The Booger.

Sometimes I would sit by the window and watch The Booger's antics and wonder why we couldn't have adopted a doe-eyed cocker spaniel or a clever border collie. Terriers were spry and full of fun. I even would have enjoyed a sort of a regal boxer to guard our home. Even though I'm a major animal lover, after a while I had a hard time seeing any redeeming qualities in this pup.

One day, feeling overwhelmed by family burdens and seeking a quiet place, I slipped out the back door into the evening solitude. I walked through the yard and sat down on the grass at the base of a mimosa tree. I drew my knees close to my chest and curled my arms around them. Then I started to cry. I poured out all the misery of a day filled with conflicts and tension.

After a few minutes, I felt something brush against my shoulder. I looked up and blinked back tears, only to see The Booger staring back at me in the twilight. Slowly he snuggled closer. He moved hesitantly, as if unsure how to go about it, but finally ended up with my arms wrapped around his neck. For over an hour, this usually squirming puppy sat silently across my lap as I told him of my troubles and cried into his fluffy coat.

The next morning, I stepped out the back door and looked around for The Booger. He was busy playing tug-of-war with a sheet hanging on the clothesline. When he saw me, he came bounding across the yard with his comical, I'm-so-dumb-I'm-proud-of-it expression, his eyes dancing and tail wagging. Same ol' Booger. Same ol' goofball style. Things hadn't changed. Well, one thing was different. From that time on, after this bouncy dog had shown such compassion to me in my time of sorrow, The Booger always held a special place in my heart.

Meditation

Is there something lovable and generous in even the most annoying person or animal in your life today? Would showing your vulnerability allow someone to become closer to you?

A Tender Solution for a Tough Problem

Lyndra Hearn Antonson
Minnetonka, Minnesota

I adopted Presty when she was already six years old. She is a springer-sheltie mix and gets very excited when her mother (me) or her father, my husband, Dale, comes home. When she gets wound up, Presty barks so loudly and frequently that it can be painful to listen to her. Shortly after I adopted her, I began trying to help her overcome the habit of barking with such enthusiasm at our arrival. I would say, "Quiet," and gently hold her snout shut.

One evening, I came in the door and Presty began to bark in her usual manner. I said, "Quiet!" She started running around the house as if she were searching for something. A few moments later, Presty came back in the room with one of her stuffed toy animals in her mouth and the rest of her body swaying with excitement. It seems that since she couldn't control her

Lyndra's Presty

110

barking, she used her intelligence, creativity, and desire to please to come up with a solution. This totally warmed my heart and increased my love for her even more.

To this day, whenever we come home, Presty greets us silently with a stuffed toy animal in her mouth while her whole body wags hello.

Meditation

What creative solutions could you find for people or situations that appear to be out of control but maybe need only a thinking-outside-the-box alternative?

Sierra, the Dog Who Taught Me
to Live in the Moment

Monique Muhlenkamp
Petaluma, California

*I*f the sounds of my worrying mind could be heard, there would be a steady stream of questions: Did I lock the door? Did I shut off the coffeepot? Is the pilot light still lit? Phrases beginning with "What if" pop into my head more often than I would like. Fortunately, I have a four-legged teacher who helps me to get past my anxiety. Her name is Sierra. She is a yellow Lab–greyhound mix whose live-in-the-moment attitude has finally won over her struggling human student.

One Saturday morning, my husband, Steve, suggested we take Sierra to the beach to let her run off some pent-up winter energy. I thought that was a great idea until I started anticipating all of the dangers that might await us at the beach.

What if Sierra saw a bird, took off after him, and never came back?

What if she ran into the ocean and got eaten by a shark? After all, the Northern California coast is white-shark territory.

What if Sierra disturbed a seal and a ranger threw us into the clink?

After plowing through my list of concerns, I finally agreed to the trip. But the closer we drove to the beach, the more worried I became. Still, I had to smile when I turned around to the backseat of our car and saw the goofy grin on my furry teacher's face. Sierra is no dummy. She knew exactly where we were going and all the delights to come. She seemed to be daydreaming about long, uninterrupted sprints along the sandy beach, jumping through white frothy waves, running after seagulls, and catching the Fris-bee. She also must have been look-

Monique's Sierra

ing forward to her favorite beach dance — the wet dog shake, all over our blanket and picnic goodies.

I started to think about Sierra's view of life and came up with a new batch of what-ifs.

What if Steve and I had a nice time watching Sierra frolic, instead of me being too focused on what could go wrong versus what could go right?

What if I took my camera out of its bag and snapped some fun action shots?

What if I just plain enjoyed myself?

And, gasp, what if I applied this more relaxed attitude to other areas of my life?

The closer we got to the ocean, the more excited Sierra became. Her joy was so contagious that it even infected me!

After we piled out of the car, I watched Sierra tear down the beach and break into the smooth lope that happens only when she has plenty of runway. It was a joyful, carefree sight to behold. I captured the rest of the unfolding day through my eyes and my camera lens. After the film was developed, it thrilled me to see that I had taken a photo that said it all. It showed Sierra plunging headlong into frothy ocean water with her ears pinned back by the wind and a big grin on her face. This vision of Sierra's freedom reminded me of the life lesson she taught me that day: *Live joyfully, and for goodness' sake, stop worrying. Life is far, far too short.*

Meditation

What is a dog trying to teach you about living in the moment and enjoying the now?

Leading the Way

Eleanor Garrell Berger
Northern New York State

*T*ycho is a very old dog — past ninety in human years. Like other ancient canines, he is both an inspiration and an expert on aging well. Moving stiffly, but without self-pity, he retains a dignity undiminished by my thoughtless impatience at having to slow down to accommodate his unfocused dawdling. Although he has his spry moments, Tycho is usually content to watch from his bed as others play the games he used to enjoy. Despite cloudy vision, conveniently diminished hearing, and degenerative disk disease, Tycho gets around quite well. In fact, very well when extra attention or a biscuit are in the offing.

On our outings, Tycho stops and sniffs endlessly as he tries to recall the identity of the dog that marked before him. I understand his challenge every time I reach into my own memory for a name to put with a familiar face. Unfortunately, I don't enjoy the mental taffy-pull as much as Tycho does. Perhaps a bit of sniffing would bolster my own recall.

In short, our standard schnauzer is a model senior citizen. If I should have the privilege of living into my nineties, I hope I remember Tycho's approach to aging, because I'd like to do it his way.

But what am I to do in the meantime, now that I'm fifty-something? Who's going to set an example for me? Lead the way? Someone middle-aged would be best. My human contemporaries, however, tend toward the exceptional, possessed of an energy of mind and flexibility of body I didn't have even at twenty. They are achiever types, successful in business and accomplished at hobbies. A more forgiving model would be more to my liking.

And I just happen to have one. A canine named Gambit. At fifty-something himself, in human years, he is doing middle age the way it should be done, with a perspective on life that I find contagious.

Eleanor's Gambit

Gambit knows how to separate the important from the unimportant. He reserves his terrier war dance for squirrels playing on his lawn and in his trees. Meanwhile, he gives a pass to crows on his deck, squirrels in the yard next door, and even chipmunks — as long as they're beyond the reach of his retractable lead. There's a lot to be said for this approach, for letting some issues go and not waging war on all fronts. At the very least, it conserves a middle-ager's energy. So, matching Gambit's spirit, I've decided to give my neighbors a "pass" on their road-littering habits and save my war dance for their all-night teenage parties.

Even after eight years of daily walking, when I pick up Gambit's lead, he yaps and jumps about, expressing his enthusiasm for the ordinary. Under his tutelage I, too, have come to appreciate the pleasures of a long walk, a cozy nest, and a simple bowl of food (especially if someone else prepares it, serves it, and washes the plate).

Now that we're in our fifties, Gambit and I are ready to focus on projects we once put aside. Gambit is becoming proficient at tracking. In his youth he was more interested in barking at other dogs than in following his nose. In my youth, too, I was interested in socializing and running about. Now, however, I prefer growing a garden, strengthening friendships, and exploring new places — with a nose-down intensity that I picked up from my friend Gambit.

Eleanor's Tycho

My terrier and I have learned to pace ourselves. We no longer rush around all day. We take time out to play. We drink more water and need to "go" more often. We ask for what we want and accept that we won't always get it. We're willing to cooperate and compromise but know when to draw the line. Gambit draws his at having his nails cut. I draw mine at eating genetically modified food.

We know what we like, and we don't like being cold and wet. We know our limits — neither of us enjoys jogging anymore. We don't worry about the past. We think we have things yet to achieve in the future. We enjoy a good stretch. We appreciate a little nap. And we like to talk with our friends, Gambit rather more loudly than I prefer.

Life is satisfying with a middle-aged dog around to share my middle years. It's pleasant having a furry friend to give direction and keep me on course. And it's a comfort knowing that, as we grow old together, we can follow in the paw prints of Tycho, our ancient canine example, who walked into his senior years ahead of us, leading the way.

Meditation

Could an aging dog be the perfect companion for an aging person? Is it always the puppies who make the most compassionate pets, or could an older, rescued dog from an animal shelter bring just the right amount of energy and gratitude you need?

Dog Day

Roberta Beach Jacobson
Karpathos Island, Greece

*W*hen I was young and growing up in northern Illinois, on one special day between Christmas and New Year's Day the dogs ruled our household. We'd pick one carefree day during that long winter week, and everyone in the family would pitch in to spoil our dogs rotten. Dog Day became a family tradition, a welcome change from the hustle and bustle of the holidays. We always played "go fetch" with our trio of dogs on the frozen lake, and before long, we'd attract a whole line of curious children tagging along with us. We'd build a snowman in the front yard and throw snowballs for the dogs to chase.

Also on Dog Day, we groomed the pooches, combing their fur and clipping their nails. One year, Mom decided that she wanted to master the dogs' grooming needs and enrolled in an evening course called "Clip Your Own Poodle." Poor Fi-Fi and Susie became her rather unwilling models. Mom never got it quite right. Not that her heart wasn't in it. But one side of their bodies always wound up shaggier or curlier than the other, and I'm sure the poodles were offended by her enthusiasm.

Another year, Mom bought a book on dog grooming to help her hone her fur-clipping skills. But it was not to be. When she tried a

French cut on Fi-Fi, we viewed Fi-Fi's skin for the first time. She had huge pink spots, not unlike a pig. Charlie, the lucky dog, was a short-haired mutt. This meant he was spared my mother's haircuts and only got brushed.

On Dog Day we took the doggies in the car no matter where we went on errands. The dogs wore their matching plaid jackets on all of the outings. After all, this was their day! Dad made sure that there would be juicy bones for each of the dogs. For Fi-Fi and Susie, this treat was really worth wagging their tails about. Charlie, who lived to be eleven, would eat just about anything. As if on cue, he'd take his Dog Day bone and try to bury it near the snowman, but the ground was always, alas, frozen solid.

Roberta's Susie and Fi-Fi

Some years the neighborhood kids would show up with their canines on Dog Day. We'd all hike for miles around the lake, slipping and sliding half the way. The dogs tried to run on the ice, but their feet often would not cooperate. Sometimes we'd take black-and-white pictures of our antics. We'd come back from the walks feeling exhausted and carting bags of pinecones, unusual rocks, and whatever interesting items we had found along the way that weren't frozen to the ground.

Our family always consisted of three people and three dogs. Over time, as dog members of the family changed, we'd add a few innovations to the annual celebration. One year, all the dogs got new collars. Another year they received red squeaky toys that we threw around in the snow. All of the toys got lost that Dog Day. We simply could not find the little toys in the deep Illinois snowdrifts. We probably didn't stay in one spot long enough to keep track of them, either.

Nobody in our family could remember who dreamed up the Dog Day idea, but it seemed as if we'd always celebrated it. It was our way of relaxing and making sure every dog had his day.

Meditation

Would you like to host a Dog Day for your neighborhood or family? What special treats could humans and dogs enjoy together for your Dog Day?

Taylor Teaches Us How to Play

Allen Anderson
Minneapolis, Minnesota

*M*y wife, Linda, and I lead very busy and often stressful lives. We work hard, travel often, and spend whatever time we have outside of our day jobs working on projects for our Angel Animals Network. Sometimes, play seems not to fit into our lifestyle.

One day in June, Linda had just returned to Minneapolis from California after consulting with a book-coaching client out there. Since we have four pets, we try to arrange our schedules so one of us is always home. This has meant that sometimes Linda's arrival corresponds with my departure. So it was a treat on this summer afternoon to pick up my wife from the airport and know that we'd have a few days to spend together.

On the way home we began talking about Linda's client and how difficult it had been to accomplish in five days what should have taken two weeks. We also discussed my latest business trip, upcoming travel, and the looming deadline for our second book proposal. In only one hour, we had managed to make ourselves feel overwhelmed by all we needed to do.

At home, our animal family greeted us warmly. Taylor, our yellow Labrador retriever, wagged her tail hard, thumping it against the wall. As if sensing what we needed, she ran into my office and found the yellow tennis ball that I always use to play catch with her. We looked at Taylor with the tennis ball in her mouth, then at each other. Linda said, "Let's take a break before we go back to work. Why don't we walk by the lake and have some Adele's frozen custard?" Those were the magic words — Adele's frozen custard. Adele's is a Minnesota classic, a place in Excelsior that serves one of our, and Taylor's, favorite treats.

Off we went with Taylor in the backseat of our car to Adele's and Lake Minnetonka. Sensing something fun was about to happen, the dog squealed all the way. She'd shift from one side of the car to the other in anticipation of which way we were going to turn. We were so amused by Taylor's joy that we forgot to talk about all the things on our to-do lists. Along with our carefree and playful dog, we took delight in imagining a tennis ball, a lake, a place to run free, and of course, a frozen custard treat.

By the time we arrived at the lake, the afternoon had turned into a beautiful summer evening, with fading sunlight gleaming off the water's surface. We stopped at Adele's and bought three custards — two in cups and one in a cone, for Taylor. We laughed, watching her eat with gusto as she slathered custard all over her mouth and the car's upholstery. We didn't mind the mess. It was entertaining to watch her have so much fun slurping the gooey vanilla with her big, pink tongue.

As we walked along the lakeside with a gentle breeze cooling us, we began to release all the ups and downs, the heavy conversations, and the anxiety of the week. I threw the tennis ball, and Taylor carefully climbed over the slippery rocks along the shore, jumped into the water, and swam out to retrieve it. Fishing the bobbing yellow ball out of the water is a game Taylor can play endlessly, and it soon became mechanical for me to throw it and let her swim back and forth.

While we waited on the shore for Taylor to return, our conversation drifted back to work, and we began to talk chores again. What had been a stress-free outing was quickly slipping into agitation over all of our responsibilities and concerns. Soon we were telling each other that we must return to the car and go home to work, or we'd never get everything finished. I stopped throwing the ball and signaled for Taylor to come with us.

Allen and Linda's Taylor

But she would have none of this disruption of her playtime. Without hesitation, Taylor knocked the ball from my hand, ran with it in her mouth to the lake's edge, swung her head, and threw the ball into the water as far as she could. Then she gave us a look as if to say, "This is what *you're* supposed to do." She swam for the ball, brought it back to where we were standing, and dropped it at my feet. Her eyes said it all: "See? This is how to have fun. Your turn."

She had such sincerity in her gaze, trying in her doggy way to teach us how to play, that all we could do was laugh. Again we felt the tension drain from our bodies. Taylor was showing us that the anxiety we felt was of our own creation. Throwing the ball as far away as we could was like letting go of our attachment to the outcomes of our work. The tasks, like Taylor's tennis ball, would bounce back soon enough. Meanwhile, in her canine opinion, we needed to learn how to have more fun!

Thank goodness we have such a good teacher in Taylor. She's a master at reminding us to find and keep more balance in our lives — and at showing us how to do it.

Meditation

How are workaholic tendencies, a strong sense of responsibility, and a never-ending to-do list ruining your sense of playfulness and adventure? What could a dog teach you about balance?

Ask Taylor

Dear Taylor,

Why does my dog smile? She gets this big, goofy grin on her face like she's hearing a secret joke. What does she think is so funny?

Sincerely,

My Dog's Favorite Toy

Dear Favorite Toy,

Your dog smiles because she thinks you are the funniest thing she has ever seen. You walk on only two legs. You can hardly hear your telephone ringing in the house, much less the ice-cream truck from three blocks away. Your nose is so tender that you

actually think it's disgusting to smell a friend's,
well, you know what I mean. No wonder your dog gets
a good laugh whenever you're around.

Besides, she thinks you're the dearest creature.
You light up her world and bring the biggest smile
of all to her face.

Grinningly yours,

Taylor

Now that you're learning how to appreciate being cast in the role
of your dog's favorite toy, you'll find great satisfaction in understanding the role your dog is playing as healer. The next chapter
introduces you to some of the best doggy doctors on the planet.

CHAPTER FOUR

Are Dogs Your Divine Prescription for Better Health?

When illness forced me to shift my focus to the here and now, my pets became my physical therapists, pain management consultants, personal trainers, and psychological counselors. I only received these benefits because I took the time to enhance our Bond: to slow to their pace, follow their instincts, and begin, like them, to listen to my heart and express gratitude for simpler gifts.

— Marty Becker, *The Healing Power of Pets*

*D*ogs are kissing, tail-wagging, life-affirming healers. Through the loving eyes of a dog, people experience who they truly are underneath their worries and pain and the masks they present to the world. You can't fool a dog. Dogs know when you're sad. They sense when you need them. They are so physically in tune with their human companions, according to the veterinarian Dr. Marty Becker, that they can detect an impending heart attack, an epileptic seizure, or a drop in blood sugar.[1] In October 2004, the researcher Dr. John Church of Amersham Hospital in Amersham, England, reported a study in the *British Medical Journal* that used six dogs of various breeds to detect bladder cancer in the urine samples of thirty-six patients. The dogs correctly found the cancer twenty-two out of fifty-four times. All the dogs detected cancer in one patient who was thought to have no cancer. After more testing, the patient's medical doctors found that the man had a carcinoma in his right kidney.[2]

Edward Creagan, an oncologist at the Mayo Clinic, verifies that pets can be the missing ingredient in recovery, the crucial factor that helps a patient get well. Dr. Creagan says, "Many times, the family pet can motivate a patient to give her best effort to deal with a serious illness such as cancer. About five years ago, I began asking my patients about their pets, and it was amazing to see the smiles illuminate their faces. Today, I write down the name of pets whenever I take a medical history."[3]

Dogs help ill people recover and serve them with special attention when they are disabled. Dogs also can prevent illness. According to Texas A&M University's *Science Daily*, a study of one hundred Medicare patients showed that "senior adults who own dogs go to the doctor less [often] than those who do not."[4]

Our personal experience with dogs and health comes from receiving tender loving care from our dog, Taylor, and her lovely predecessor, a golden retriever named Prana. Both of these dogs always showed the greatest concern when either of us were feeling low; and they both required walking, which of course is wonderful for a healthy heart.

We also have witnessed the transformation a little white dog brought to the lives of Linda's parents, Gert and Darrell Jackson, when they retired to Texas. Linda's sister, Janet, gave them the gift of a miniature poodle puppy, aptly named Angel. This dog has brought so much joy to their lives. When Linda's mother had to be rushed to the hospital in an ambulance one day, Angel, her little body shaking with emotion, escaped from the yard and ran after the vehicle until Janet's husband, Mario, could scoop up Angel and carry her back home. Everyone had to spend time reassuring Angel that Linda's mother would return soon, which she thankfully did, into the loving paws of a dog who is these eighty-year-olds' constant companion.

Gert and Darrell Jackson's Angel

In this chapter you will meet remarkable dogs who have degrees as health-care specialists from Doggy Medical and Holistic Healing Universities:

- Haley, the service dog who gave a teenager the help and hope she needed to survive radiation therapy

- Boise, the Guiding Eyes for the Blind dog who made her entrance onto this planet at exactly the right time to turn darkness into light

- Oliver, a freezing, abandoned shih tzu who warmed the heart of a dying man

- Joshua B. Dawg, a rescued wise Lhasa apso–cocker mix who saved his own life through trust and patience

- Shep, an empathic dog who connected with a young man in intensive care with a startling act of devotion

- Wanda, an Irish wolfhound–terrier mix who gave her human companion the strength to be present for her father's last days

- And Taylor, who hints in "Ask Taylor" that there's more to dogs as natural healers than most people ever imagine.

If you have not recognized the healing abilities of dogs, this chapter should help you to observe what dogs are doing for you now, what they have done in the past, or how a dog in your future could be exactly the right prescription for whatever might be ailing you.

Haley, the Angel Dog Who
Helped Me through Cancer

Ashley Phelps
Bend, Oregon

J took a step into the unfamiliar office of the Central Oregon Cancer Treatment Center. I could smell the scent of hospital with a touch of home. The odors reassured me, because hospital and home were the two places where I had to spend most of my time after I got sick. I took a couple more steps and stopped to look around. My mom, frustrated with my hesitation, walked around me and went to the front desk. I quickly followed her.

I turned around and saw a waiting room with what was supposed to be sick patients filled instead with smiling, happy people. I found this a bit strange but sat down. My mom soon sat next to me with lots of papers to fill out. This is something we were used to. Since I was diagnosed with Hodgkin's lymphoma, we had doctors' appointments at least once a day.

Today's appointment was for radiation therapy, which I knew nothing about. A few minutes later, a very pretty golden retriever came around the corner. The dog followed a lady who seemed to be her handler. I was very surprised, because I had never seen a dog in a doctor's office! The dog came straight toward me and put her head on my lap. The handler looked to be okay with this, and it didn't seem harmful, so naturally I petted the dog.

The handler sat next to me and said, "This is Haley. She is the therapy dog here at the radiation clinic."

I didn't respond but nodded and kept petting the dog. Haley's handler then walked over to a clear box with drawers and pulled out a red ball. This got Haley's attention right away. I watched Haley do tricks and play with her ball. For the first time in four months, I smiled. Haley soon lost interest in her tricks and brought me a red ball that she seemed to be very fond of.

Her handler came and sat next to me again. She said, "My name is Sharen Meyers. Haley seems to like you a lot. Usually she likes most people who are younger than twenty."

Ashley's friend Haley

I looked around the room and realized that all the people in the waiting room, except for me, my mom, and Sharen, were at least over fifty. I was only thirteen and would be turning fourteen in a little over a week.

Just then, the nurse called my name. She took my mom and me into a small room to wait for the doctor. The doctor, a petite woman, came in; she was almost as small as me, and I weigh a hundred pounds. She introduced herself as Dr. Chang. She told me that she had talked to my doctors in Portland and my doctor here. The plan was for me to do fourteen days of radiation therapy. My last day would be on June 23, 2004.

After the appointment, I said good-bye to Haley and went home to rest. It had been about a week and a half since my last chemotherapy, and I still had very little energy.

I had never really been all that fond of dogs. I was kind of a cat person. But Haley seemed different and was making me think about what it would be like to have a dog for a friend.

I started radiation on the following Thursday. I was disappointed to find that Haley wasn't there. The receptionist told me that Haley came to the hospital only on Mondays, Tuesdays, and Wednesdays. I had been looking forward to seeing her. I went through the treatment and discovered that unlike what I had expected, the radiation made me sick, but not nearly as sick as chemotherapy.

I was really excited when it was time for my Monday appointment, even though I didn't look forward to the radiation. I just wanted to see Haley. The first week of radiation I had a lot of fun with Haley, watching her do tricks and playing fetch with her. She also could do hurdles. If Sharen put three cups on the ground and a treat under one of them, Haley could find the cup with the treat under it. Haley also knew how to open a mailbox and get the mail and find balls that were hidden around the room.

I could tell Haley was helping me to recover with a more positive attitude. For some reason, she made me feel like it was okay that I had cancer and was always sick. When I played with Haley, it didn't matter that I had no hair or that I had to stop going to school. When I was with Haley, I didn't feel different from other kids. She made me feel like I was welcome and belonged somewhere — that it was okay to be different, because she was a friend to me.

The second week of my radiation therapy, Sharen asked me if I would like to learn how to train Haley and help her. I said, "Yes, of course!" So for the rest of my radiation treatments, on every Monday, Tuesday, and Wednesday, Sharen taught me a lot about training. She showed me how to use a clicker and click it at the exact moment when Haley was doing what we wanted and then to give her a treat as a reward. Sharen also taught me how dogs think and that they are very aware of what's going on around them. These were things that I didn't realize.

Soon I was able to help Sharen and Haley in the clinic. Every Monday and Wednesday, after I was finished with my treatment, Haley and Sharen would set up for whatever trick we were working on at the time, usually hurdles. I gained Haley's trust by giving her commands or playing fetch and teaching her how to sink a basketball into a basket.

On my last day of therapy, the doctor gave me a certificate for finishing radiation treatment. Everyone had signed it, including Sharen and Haley, with her paw print. Sharen gave me her card and told me to call and let her know if I wanted to come in and train Haley during the summer. I told her I would call as soon as possible. I wasn't expecting my summer to be very busy.

Because of the time I spent with Haley and the way she helped me to feel happier, I had a much better attitude. I was able to go back to school. I even graduated from middle school that year. And as it turned out, I was wrong about the summer; it was very busy. So busy, in fact, that I never called Sharen. I thought about it all summer and wanted to see her and Haley very much. But I was enjoying the summer, visiting family, and spending time with friends. I was never able to do all those things while I was sick. I loved being a teenager again.

When the summer was over, I went to high school. I felt guilty about not going to see Haley, but I had an appointment for a checkup at the radiation clinic one Friday. Knowing Haley would not be there on Friday, I intended to leave Haley and Sharen a note to let them know about my summer and that I missed them a lot.

On the day of the appointment, I waited after school for my mom to come home. The appointment was at four o'clock. My mom was late and didn't get home until four-thirty, so she called to reschedule my appointment. Luckily it would be on Monday. I was really excited and couldn't wait to see Haley!

Monday finally came around, and my mom picked me up from school. As we pulled up to the hospital, I had a funny feeling and didn't want to go into the office. But my excitement overruled this feeling. I went inside, sat down, and waited for Haley to come running up to me as she had so many times before. I looked around and noticed that Haley's box wasn't there. I hoped it had only been moved. Inside, I knew what must have happened. I just couldn't accept it. My mom was sitting next to me. She asked the receptionist if Haley was there today. I wanted to cover my ears.

The woman sighed and said, "I am sorry to tell you this, but Haley passed away a couple of months ago. She had major thyroid problems and was on medication. One day, she was lying there by the door and didn't want to get up or anything. I'm very sorry."

My mom said, "Oh, that's so sad."

I just sat there, stunned, and wondering how this could have happened. My eyes got watery. I thought about the first time I met

Haley, and how she had put her head on my lap. I remembered all the times I helped her with her work and how happy she made me feel on the days I could barely get out of bed. I tried not to cry. But being in this place with all my memories of Haley, it was unbearable to know that she was gone. I remembered her coming around the very same corner I had been sitting next to and making all the people in the waiting room smile.

As I think about it now, I realize that Haley was an angel. She helped me and many other people get through the hardest times in our lives. I will never forget how much she helped me.

Meditation

Is there a dog to whom you want to express gratitude for helping you heal and recover? If this dog has passed on, could you honor him or her in some way with a tribute, memorial, or even a letter you write to say how much you appreciate those blessings?

More about Haley

Sharen Meyers
Bend, Oregon

*B*efore my beautiful golden retriever, Haley, met thirteen-year-old Ashley Phelps at the Central Oregon Cancer Treatment Center, this dog had a remarkable history. It brought her to the time and place where she could work with me to give that special therapy only a dog can deliver.

Haley's journey in service to life began when people abandoned her and her five-day-old litter of golden retriever–Lab puppies at the back door of a "kill" animal pound in Cincinnati, Ohio. Circle Tail, Inc., found Haley and her pups at the pound and adopted them. Circle Tail is a nationwide organization that, in coordination with the Pet Prison Partnership Program, trains service dogs. Circle Tail volunteers go to city pounds and shelters to find dogs who are suitable for service training. These dogs are entered into their training program to work as service therapy dogs.

When Haley's puppies were eight weeks old, Circle Tail found homes for each one of them. Then they assigned Haley to the Pet Prison Partnership Program. At the time Haley was being brought into the prison training program, I worked for the Kendall County Health and Human Services Department, which was starting a dog therapy program for the county. The three prisons that participate in training service dogs send the graduated dogs to a place they call the "dog farm." Haley and I met at the dog farm, and we really bonded. I adopted Haley to be my therapy service dog, and we spent a weekend getting to know each other and learning how to work together.

Haley went through additional training and was certified as a therapy dog. All anyone had to do was look at Haley, and it was obvious she would be great at therapy work. Her face was full of emotion. She had so much love to give.

Since I am a social worker, I had Haley work with me to help teens who had behavioral and self-control problems. They learned how to build a relationship with Haley through positive reinforcement, tolerance, and other positive attributes. Haley served as the perfect mirror for teens. She gave them love when they did the right things. If they misbehaved, she ignored them. These troubled teenagers learned from Haley's example. Haley loved teenagers. It was as if she knew her job was to help young people. She did not pay much attention to adults or older people.

Recently Haley and I moved from Illinois to Oregon. That is how we met Ashley at the cancer treatment center, where I was bringing Haley to do therapy work with the patients. Normally, in the clinic waiting room, I would signal Haley to visit someone who I thought might need attention. The day that Haley and Ashley met and started their friendship was the first time Haley did not wait for a signal from me. When Haley saw Ashley in the waiting room, she ran over and laid her head in Ashley's lap. Then she looked into the girl's eyes. Haley wouldn't move. She kept her head on Ashley's lap for a long time and later maintained focused eye contact with the girl.

Haley was so caring toward Ashley, it was as if this dog wanted to be Ashley's mother, as well as her friend. Ashley seemed to be very sensitive. Haley also was sensitive. The two immediately bonded. Haley would come alive whenever she saw Ashley. Every visit, Haley singled out Ashley to befriend. Through Ashley's entire series of radiation treatments, Haley stayed with her. After Ashley left each time, Haley would fall into a very deep and sound sleep.

Sharen's Haley

With each visit, especially after Ashley started learning how to train Haley, I marveled at the lessons that this dog was teaching to a young girl who faced high hurdles. In addition to physical recovery, Ashley had to overcome the other obstacles that illness had placed in her way and re-enter life as a teenager again. For instance, sometimes Haley didn't feel like jumping over hurdles or didn't want to jump as high as we had placed the hurdle. I never forced Haley to jump but respected her wish not to follow through on a command. At those times, if we lowered the hurdle, Haley would jump over it. This showed that Haley wasn't being stubborn. Instead, she knew her own day-to-day limitations and understood not to exceed them. By my having a nonjudgmental attitude and accepting that Haley had more wisdom about herself than I did, Ashley may have learned to follow her own wisdom in regard to how much she should push herself each day of her recovery.

Sometimes, when we went outside to throw the ball, Haley would get distracted by all the fresh scents. I think that also was good for Ashley to see, because Haley thoroughly enjoyed being alive, going outside, and exploring new experiences. Haley was always very curious about everything, including what was in peoples' purses, diaper bags, etc. I think Haley's love for life gave Ashley permission to rejoin life as a fourteen-year-old and enjoy living once again. Haley's lessons to all of us were to live life to the fullest and accept love.

Haley had a hypothyroid problem, but medication was helping her with that. On the morning of her death, she seemed fine after our walk and showed no signs of illness. Apparently, she died from a heart problem. It was as if her big and generous heart had just stopped beating.

When Allen and Linda Anderson contacted me to say that Ashley Phelps had sent them a story about Haley, I was surprised. At the clinic, Ashley did not say more than six words throughout all of her visits. She was a very shy teenager. I hadn't expected this quiet high-school girl to express herself so eloquently.

After Allen and Linda sent me the story, I read it to the staff at the cancer treatment center. With tears in our eyes, we all appreciated taking a few minutes to hear Ashley's tribute to Haley, the dog who loved her so much and who helped so many people through their struggles with cancer.

Meditation

When have you felt like one of life's throwaways or rejects? How could Haley's remarkable generosity inspire you to find the strength and ability in yourself that would allow you to serve and to thrive?

Note: Since Haley and Ashley made such a strong healing bond, you may want to know about an organization that specializes in connecting dogs with those whose lives are affected by cancer. Paws for a Cure is a national charity fund-raiser in which families, friends, and cancer survivors walk with their dogs and raise money to benefit the National Childhood Cancer Foundation. This organization is rated A+ by the American Institute of Philanthropy and dedicates more than 94 percent of its total expenditures to finding cures for children with cancer. For more information or to make a donation, visit www.pawswalk.org or write to the National Childhood Cancer Foundation, P.O. Box 60012, Arcadia, CA 91066-6012, or call (800) 458-6223.

Angel in Waiting

Sally Rosenthal
Philadelphia, Pennsylvania

"Are you really blind?" asked the elderly man as he grasped my hand while Boise rested her soft Labrador muzzle on the nursing home resident's lap. A sweet, caring soul, my guide dog took her pet therapy work seriously and never overlooked an opportunity to dispense her special brand of charm and concern.

My positive response to the man's question made him cry, until I reminded him that the dog he was caressing took good care of me. He grasped my hand more tightly but calmed as he realized I was right. We sat, for the moment connected in our separate difficulties by Boise, my angel who wore her wings proudly, even if they were hidden by a soft black coat of fur.

I was not surprised by my exchange with the gentleman, because in the year and a half we have been a team, Boise has specialized in connecting me to individuals as well as to the world at large. It is no small task, I admit, but Boise, as I have come to realize, is no ordinary dog.

Most of the people who see us on the street as we go about our daily business view a guide dog like Boise as a source of independence, an alternative method of getting around for those of us who are blind. While I cannot argue with their perception, I have to acknowledge that the independence Boise affords me, as important as it is, is not her most valuable contribution to my well-being. With her friendly Labrador demeanor, Boise has led me to people and activities that I, somewhat isolated by blindness, might not have otherwise encountered.

Losing my sight slowly over twenty years had presented many challenges, but the hardest of them occurred five years ago, during the few months when my remaining vision slipped away. In that difficult winter, my father died after a long battle with kidney cancer, and my husband was seriously injured in an accident. Pocus, one of our beloved cats, died sud-denly as a result of heart disease. When I became totally blind during that time, I thought the world had become a dark place, literally and metaphorically. In addition to losing self-confidence, I felt as though I were losing connections to people and the world beyond my front door.

A guide dog might, I surmised, make me more independent and serve as an "icebreaker" with people who tended to shy away from blind-ness. I applied to Guiding Eyes for the Blind in Yorktown Heights, New

Sally and Boise

York, and waited to be matched with a canine partner. When I trained and began working with Boise, I realized how right my assumptions had been. Interested strangers stopped us to admire Boise and ask questions. Shopkeepers became more helpful, small children everywhere were enamored of my guide, and Boise became the canine celebrity of the church I joined. The family who raised Boise as a puppy for Guiding Eyes became my good friends. Boise and I became pet therapy volunteers and made new friends through Internet guide-dog handlers' groups. In fact, several of my Internet friends sent us dog bandannas that Boise wears to charm patients, such as the elderly gentleman, with whom we feel a sense of kinship.

Most guide dogs serve similar roles of providing independence, mobility, and socialization for their human partners. It wasn't until I considered Boise's birth date that I realized she is truly an angel. She was, I learned, born in April, the same month that my dark winter had turned to spring. Unbeknownst to me at that time, a small, living bundle of black fur had come into the world with the purpose of guiding my feet and my spirit. Boise, the dog who comforted my nursing home friend so well, had begun her life on earth as an angel in waiting. She continues to take each chance to remind me just how well she has assumed her mission through her work in harness as a guide dog and the joy she brings to me and others.

As we left the nursing home, Boise nudged me as if to remind me that, in all our dark times, angels are often lurking, waiting for the right moment to come into the light.

Meditation

Was an angel dog being born during a time when you were going through a tough period? How did that dog find his or her way to you? Do you detect a divine hand guiding a dog to be a healing agent for your physical pain or depression?

How a Freezing Dog Warmed Our Hearts

Marion T. Cochrane
Northport, New York

*O*n a freezing, rainy evening during the winter of 1991, I was driving to our local market when I slammed on the brakes to avoid hitting a little black-and-white something that was running in circles in front of my car. I jumped out of the car to take a closer look, and there he was, in the middle of the intersection, a shivering mess of canine with his coat covered in ice. At the same time that I stopped, another driver approached the scene. This driver thought that the dog belonged to me, and I in turn thought the same of him. After we exchanged wonderment over how this little creature had survived on the city road, the other driver proceeded on his way.

I picked up the little dog, wrapped him in a blanket that I keep in my car, and went into the market to see if anyone recognized the little fellow. No one did.

Since no one was on the darkening streets looking for their lost pet, I decided to take the dog home with me. All the way, this little guy kept trying to climb out of the blanket and onto my lap to lick my face. It felt as if he were very grateful that I had rescued him.

My husband, Tom, and I named this little shih tzu Oliver. The dog reminded me of his namesake in the novel *Oliver Twist*: the little boy left orphaned to survive in a cruel world. I took the dog to visit our vet, Dr. Jonathan Greenfield at the Syosset Animal Hospital, and was relieved to find out that Oliver was rather healthy in spite of his ordeal. My husband and I placed an ad in the "lost and found" section of several local newspapers, but no one called about Oliver. After waiting for two weeks to get a response to our ad, we decided to welcome Oliver into our family, which also included two golden retrievers, Molly and Fagan.

Oliver came home with me during a period that was especially difficult. Tom was in chemotherapy. Throughout these rough days, perky little Oliver would jump up on the bed after Tom's treatments and snuggle next to him, while Molly and Fagan took up residence on either side on the floor. With their watchful eyes, the threesome seemed to know instinctively that their welcomed presence comforted my husband. Oliver would amuse Tom with his antics. The dog tossed his toys to Tom and ran around in circles, panting in merriment, waiting for Tom to toss the toys back. Oliver had a calming effect on the entire household. He was a joy to behold and kept our spirits up when everything felt as if it were coming apart.

Oliver turned out to be both a joy and a godsend, on loan to us for a short time. Sadly, I lost Tom in September of 1992, and Oliver began to decline after Tom's death. I know in my heart that Oliver was an angel, sent to us as a guide and example of happy patience. While our little dog was ill, he would lie quietly as I nervously administered his medication through injections, apologizing to him all the while. During this ordeal, Oliver never displayed aggression or ill temper toward me. He would just look at me with those soft eyes that said,

"I know you are just trying to help me." Oliver passed away in December of the same year I lost Tom.

There are angels all around, and they come in all shapes and sizes. Some angels even have four legs. Now, these many years later, I know that Tom, Oliver, Molly, and Fagan have all found each other again over the Rainbow Bridge.

Meditation

Who needs to know that he or she hasn't been abandoned? If you reached out to offer your help, would you find hidden treasure among the ruins of a hurting person's life?

Joshua B. Dawg's Lamp of Faith

Patti Cole
New Bern, North Carolina

*D*uring his lightning-quick ten years as part of our lives, Joshua B. Dawg proved many times to be a wise, gentle angel and teacher. From his loving presence, I learned faith and learned to trust that the perfect outcome of any situation is assured — even though it might not be evident to me at the moment. And always, but always, my Joshua was a best friend.

I rescued Joshua, an adorable Lhasa apso–cocker mix, from a Michigan animal shelter at the fifty-ninth minute of the twenty-third hour before his looming euthanasia. But it often turned out that it was he who rescued me. Many were the times that his kind, loving gaze or his playful nuzzle or the feel of his cold, wet nose pulled me back from the edge of an emotional precipice during rough times.

But, of course, such is always the way of angel dogs. Take the business with the lamp, for example.

The day began like most any other Fourth of July in North Carolina: hot and humid. My husband, Kevin, and I had not had much fun for quite a while because of career and financial challenges. Earlier in the week, I had resolved that we needed to relax, and coincidentally, a flyer had appeared in the mailbox that very day, advertising a local

Fourth of July parade and festivities, including free food and beverages. The event was just three days away, and it would take place a few blocks from our home.

I showed Kevin the flyer. "How about this?"

He looked it over. "Sounds good. Price is right."

So we made plans to attend the parade.

I have a low tolerance for hot, muggy weather. My Michigan-bred internal cooling system simply cannot handle it. I become overheated easily. So when July Fourth dawned hot and humid, with temperatures forecast to reach ninety-five degrees, I had serious second thoughts about attending the parade. Kevin and I talked about it and decided to forge ahead in the interest of advancing the elusive notion of "fun." We reasoned that we could drive, instead of walk, the short distance to the event. I'm smart enough to know when to call it quits while outdoors. We could always come home if the heat got to be too much.

The plan was for Joshua and our other two dogs, Samantha (a.k.a. Littlebit) and Zoey, to remain at home in air-conditioned comfort. Kevin and I set off in the car in plenty of time to arrive for the parade, which was scheduled to start at 10:30 in the morning, and find a good vantage point from which to watch it. Because this is a small community, we didn't expect a crowd, or much competition for a parking or parade-watching space.

How wrong we were! As we turned the corner at the end of our street, we saw the traffic jam around Town Hall. The knot of pedestrian and vehicular traffic was putting a strain on our small police department. Lots and lots of people lined the parade route.

"We should have walked," I said to Kevin.

"Too hot."

"Well, even if we find a parking place, we might get trapped there for hours."

"Yeah, you're right." Kevin wheeled the car into a driveway and waited for an opening so he could put the car in reverse and head for home. Within moments, we were back in our driveway.

As often happens, I started to flip-flop on my decision. I turned to Kevin and said, "Maybe we should have stayed at the parade."

He paused and then said, "I'll leave it up to you."

Suddenly, although I could not explain why, I felt an urgent need to go back into our house immediately. I have learned to recognize that still, small voice inside of me. I don't always heed it, but I have learned to recognize it.

"I need to get inside," I said.

The conviction in my voice surprised me and startled Kevin. We scrambled out of the car and entered the house through the front door, as usual.

And, as usual, Zoey, our shih tzu–cocker mix, bounded to meet us at the door. Close on Zoey's dewclaws was Littlebit, scuttling toward us like a Yorkshire water bug: her little legs moved so fast that they were a blur. Was it my imagination, or did their greeting bear an unaccustomed agitation, a sense of unease?

Usually, Joshua, with seniority among our canines, was a distant third on the greeting team. This time, however, Josh didn't appear.

As I stepped into the living room, I saw the reason, and my heart caught in my throat. There, against a wall, sat my wonderful, gentle Mr. Dawg entangled in a lamp cord. The cord was wrapped around his neck, his shoulder, and down his left front leg. I froze for a moment while the tableau registered. The look in Joshua's eyes said: I hoped you would come back. I can't seem to figure this one out by myself.

Still holding my breath, I walked over to Josh, sat on the floor next to him, and stroked his head. I could not untangle the cord right away. One end of it was still plugged in to the wall outlet. The other end was attached to a heavy brass lamp that balanced precariously on the edge of a table directly over Josh's head. For reasons unknown to me — but for which I am grateful — the lamp had not yet fallen from the table.

Patti's Joshua B. Dawg

While I sat on the floor, stroking Josh's head with one hand and bracing the unstable lamp with the other, Kevin crawled under the table to pull the plug out of the wall outlet. He struggled with it for several seconds, because it was tightly plugged into a timer. As Kevin worked on the plug, Joshua sat ever so still, looking from one of us to the other, being his calm, loving, knowing self. Eventually, Kevin got the plug out.

After we unwrapped the cord from our precious furry child, both Kevin and I realized this incident could have had a much different — and very tragic — outcome. Because the plug was so tightly connected to the timer, it probably wouldn't have given way if Josh had pulled on the cord. Had Josh moved, the heavy lamp could have fallen on him. Had he struggled to extricate himself from the cord, he might have strangled on it.

Everyone in the room — a room to which normalcy had been restored — seemed to sense that angels had prevailed that day. As we sat on the floor, holding Josh close and stroking him, Littlebit made her way to us with uncharacteristic humility. Zoey pawed at our legs and arms in a way that bespoke sisterly concern. The room's atmosphere was heavy with tragedy-averted gratitude.

As Kevin ran a hand along Mr. Dawg's back, he looked Joshua in the eye and said, "Buddy, I don't know what we would do without you." Josh looked into Kevin's eyes and then looked at me, then back at Kevin. Even though I am not a professional animal communicator, I could hear Josh communicating to us today: "I wasn't worried, Mom and Dad. I knew you would come back to help. I had faith."

I told Kevin what Josh had communicated. Tears started shining in my husband's eyes. I reached out, and as Josh licked my hand, I said, "You always know, don't you? You know your mom and dad don't always listen to their 'voices.'"

"True," Josh communicated to me, "but I'm glad you listened this time."

Meditation

Have there been times when patience and trust would have brought the help or good fortune that you needed? What would happen if you listened more closely to the quiet inner voice that calls to you through the din of daily life?

Shep's Connection with Andy

Bina Aitchison Robinson and A. M. Robinson

Swain, New York

*B*INA: On September 2, 1976, I was up late, watching the presidential debate on television. Shep, a mostly collie, medium-size dog we had adopted as a pup from a family that didn't want him, lay beside me. During a stalled period, when the sound was lost on the television, Shep suddenly began to move around as if he were in agony.

Thinking he might have been seized with abdominal cramps, I let him outside, but he remained at the door. I brought him back into the house and tried unsuccessfully to comfort him. Shep was running through the house, barking and whining loudly enough to have awakened my daughter Janet. She heard me talking to him, however, and didn't get up. About twenty minutes later, the phone rang. It was a nurse calling from the emergency room of the hospital in a neighboring city. She was saying that our son, Andy, had been badly hurt in an automobile accident.

I forgot about poor Shep as I woke up my husband. We took off for the hospital, where we could only watch helplessly while Andy, blue and struggling, was fitted with a tracheal tube to restore the airway that had become blocked because of a severe head injury. Later that night, we followed our local volunteer ambulance to a major

155

medical center that was an hour-and-a-half's drive away. We stayed overnight, while the staff continued trying to save our son's life.

For two days, we stayed at the hospital, which was seventy miles from our home. Our neighbors came over to our house daily; they and our teenagers took care of Shep.

Through the week of our son's stay in the hospital, our other children told us that as Andy started recovering, Shep became more relaxed. One day, when we were home for a short time, we noticed that Shep's face still looked troubled but no longer panic-stricken, and he wasn't cringing with pain anymore.

Andy and Bina's Shep

ANDY: Shep and I were always very close. We used to take long trail walks in a place near our house called Rattlesnake Hill. One time, Shep ran off ahead of me, and I couldn't find him. I took his favorite toy and walked all around the trail, making the toy squeak so Shep would hear it. As it started getting dark, I continued to search. Finally Shep came out of the woods and plowed into me with such a look of gratitude in his eyes. I knew that Shep must have been scared and lost. But at that moment, I also knew this dog and I were insepar-able. That's why I wasn't too surprised when my parents told me how Shep had reacted by writhing in pain at the same time that I was in my car accident.

After my accident, I wanted to help Shep to relax, so I asked to have a Kleenex tucked under my arm while I was in intensive care. Then my parents took home the tissue with my scent on it.

BINA: As soon as I gave the Kleenex with Andy's scent on it to Shep, he snatched it and ran upstairs with it in his mouth. My girls said that Shep slept on the tissue each night while Andy was gone.

When our son had his first brief period of consciousness, we told him to think of Shep and send the dog a telepathic message that he was going to be okay. It was hard for Andy to do this. He was still wired up in intensive care. But Shep apparently got Andy's message, because when we came home, he had stopped running up and down the stairs all the time.

Later, Andy told our daughter Jeannie that as he drifted in and out of consciousness, he could see Shep at home, waiting for him.

ANDY: On the day I came home from the hospital, Shep waited outside for our car to arrive. When he saw us, he ran up to the car and howled with joy. He barked and barked. Then, as if to make sure we all knew that I belong to him, Shep left his scent on me by peeing on my pants leg!

BINA: Andy wrapped his arms around a joyful Shep. The ordeal they had shared was over for both of them.

ANDY: I had always called Shep by the nickname of Stu. No reason, just something I did. This name was a unique thing we had between us.

Now I'm a grown man and own a restaurant. About three years ago, someone brought a dog to me while I was at work. Shep, of course, had passed away by then. To my amazement, this dog looked exactly like Shep, with the exact same expression in his eyes. I immediately adopted the stray dog.

Every once in a while, I forget that I'm not talking to my old friend Shep and call the new dog by Shep's nickname, Stu. I guess we're still connected in that special and memorable way.

Meditation

What dogs have connected with you in ways that are both mystical and life giving? Could a soul in a dog's body have returned to you through the golden threads of love that keep you together forever?

Wanda, My Angel and Therapist

Deborah Straw
Burlington, Vermont

*A*s an only child with healthy parents I did not see much debilitating illness or death close up when I was young. Our extended family is geographically widely spread, so I didn't witness any relatives dying. The grandparent to whom I was the closest died in a Vermont hospital while I lived in Europe.

For the first time, I am watching someone die — my dad, at age eighty-nine, is coming to the end of his life. He's had emphysema for three years and is progressively weakening. On hospice care at home, Dad's shutting down — he's not eating, he's on a morphine pump attached to his thigh, and he's dependent on a catheter. It's no longer indecent for me to see him this way; we have no false modesty. Nurses come and go all day and stay the night. Dad can't open his left eye and only occasionally opens his right. His worry lines and wrinkles are disappearing, as the hospice workers told us always happens. He does still hear us; we know by his expressions, especially by his raised eyebrows when someone speaks.

During his final weeks, Dad's been able to stay at home because it's what he wanted, because it's what Mom wanted, and because the home-health and hospice care were available free of charge. Mom always promised Dad that he'd never go to a nursing home, and she's making good on that promise.

I've only seen our cats or dogs — Misty, Annie, Bauhaus — die, when, at the vet's office, we've complied in stopping their pain. This watching of a human death has been stressful and moving. I'm so glad Dad is almost done with his sick body; he's more relaxed, almost peaceful.

Through this sad time, I have been reconsidering what an angel may be. The one I want to praise here is our puppy, Wanda the Bearded Lady. When my husband and I adopted Wanda at a rural

shelter, we thought she was a short-haired Lab-terrier mix. As she grew, she developed a beard, long legs, and longer hair, heavily flecked with gray. We now think she's primarily Irish wolfhound and terrier, and we think she's finished growing.

Wanda comes everywhere with me. I've taken to calling her my therapy dog. Extremely affectionate, stubborn, and playful, Wanda has been one of my biggest solaces while

Deborah's Wanda

I stay with Dad. Now Wanda and I are nearing the end of our vigil; soon we can go home. The nurses have given Dad twenty-four hours to live.

It consoles me that this dog is a licker and a leaner, both of which warm my heart. Wanda makes me realize that there are still reasons to feel hopeful, to laugh. During this final vigil, Wanda has provided comic relief and love. To see our puppy searching under furniture for crumbs, rolling immodestly on her back, or ardently watching birds outside the window are welcome diversions. On one of our walks, Wanda picked up a large pinecone and carried it by its stem. She's so present and unself-conscious.

My love of all creatures comes from both parents. Dad grew up on a dairy farm, where he worked with draft horses and fed barn cats. He and Mom have always had pets — a rabbit named Buster, cats, two Boston terriers. Dad once nursed two red squirrels back to health, and until his illness, he fed chickadees from his bare hands.

For the last six years, my parents have lived with Franky, a yellow cat with piercing blue eyes. Generally quite aloof, as Dad became increasingly chair-bound, Franky grew more attentive and affectionate. My dad never liked TV and in the last few months has no longer been able to read. But until last week, with his cat on his lap, Dad could watch the chickadees or sparrows on the feeders and carry on short conversations with visitors.

Two of the last distinguishable words Dad uttered were "pussy cat," a request to bring Franky to his bed. With stiffened hands and energy pulled up from nowhere, Dad petted the confused and frightened cat.

Unfortunately, he didn't get to know Wanda well. Although my husband, Bruce, and I have had Wanda for nine months, Dad has been seriously ill for most of that time. For a few months, he did like to pet Wanda's bristly black hair. If Dad had wanted, our dog would have slept with him, but his hospital bed is narrow, its bars are generally up, and forty-nine-pound Wanda likes to snuggle.

While I'm waiting here at my parents' home, Wanda has slept with me on the bed, something that she is forbidden to do at my house. I need a warm body near me. Bruce is at home, going to his job until the day I call and say that it's time to come to us. Wanda has stayed silent and calm during my frequent naps, and she's adapted to playing less; I just don't have the energy.

So I've decided Wanda may indeed be an angel with furry wings. She's calmed my spirits and brought part of my home with me while I'm here. I can't wait to get home — maybe that's how Dad feels. He has his parents and nine brothers and sisters waiting somewhere for him to join them, and two weeks ago, he told my mother he'd wait for her.

As I'm sitting vigil for Dad, I read a lot. I've discovered my attention span isn't strong enough to become immersed in a novel. Instead, I'm reading short chapters in two books. One is *Final Gifts*, a hospice gift book for my mother. The case studies of dying people help me to get through this difficult passage. They assure me we're doing all the right things for my father. They give me courage.

Equally nourishing is the thick anthology *Intimate Nature: The Bond between Women and Animals*. In an essay called "First People," Linda Hogan, a Chickasaw writer, notes that animals "are our helpers and healers.... We have asked for, and sometimes been given, if we lived well enough, carefully enough, their extraordinary powers of endurance and vision, which we have added to our own knowledge, powers, and gifts when we are not strong enough for the tasks required of us."[5] I can't say better what Wanda has done for me during this period of deep grieving and letting go. I know Dad would have appreciated this dog's love and sense of humor, too.

A postscript to this story: My father, Donald Straw, died in 1998. Wanda is now eight, still a licker and a leaner and a wee bit heavier. She is still endowing me with her extraordinary powers of endurance and vision.

Meditation

When has a dog endowed you with "extraordinary powers of endurance and vision"?

Ask Taylor

Dear Taylor,

Service dogs helping the disabled, dogs licking
tears, dogs detecting diseases -- why are all of you
such natural healers?

Sincerely,
Baffled but Grateful

Dear Baffled but Grateful,

It's going to take humans a lot more time to chew on
all the ways dogs are helping and healing them.
We're patient, though, especially with patients. Get
it? Wag, wag. Bet you didn't know that dogs like
puns. Laughter is good for the soul.

The bigger question, rather than what we can do, is why do we want to serve? The answer, of course, is that we do it all for love!

Earnestly yours,

Taylor

If you're like us, this chapter gives you much to ponder about the awesome healing capabilities of dogs that allow them to be divine messengers who deliver hope and assistance to those who need it most, when they need it most.

In the next chapter you will find dogs continuing to bring spiritual gifts to grieving people who needed to know without a doubt that love never dies.

CHAPTER FIVE

Have Dogs Discovered the Doorways to Heaven?

Thus with the dog's guiding help, and with him as the focal point for the experience, I was receiving priceless primary lessons in the cosmic art of seeing things as they really are — through the mists and barriers that seem to separate all of us from one another.

— J. Allen Boone, *Kinship with All Life*

Recognition of the spiritual roles that dogs play in the lives of humans has been long in coming during these modern times. According to a press release from the Religion Writers organization (a national organization of journalists and writers who focus on religion), clergy from Lutheran, Episcopalian, Anglican, Methodist, United Church of Christ, and Roman Catholic denominations are performing the blessing of the animals on the Feast of St. Francis. Members of the clergy are also conducting memorial services for animals who have died, and sanctifying ground to be used as pet cemeteries. The theology of the divine origin of animals, and the reverence for animals as spiritual beings, both have ancient roots. The Religion

Writers press release notes, "Buddhism regards animals as beings in different stages of reincarnation. Hinduism and Jainism embrace vegetarianism out of respect for all life. Islam teaches respect for animals as part of God's creation."[1]

Even though animal blessings and the attendance of animals at church services have become more commonplace, religious dogma often clashes, quite emotionally, with the experiences of people who believe in or have experienced the afterlife of animals. To help bridge that gap, the artist Stephen Huneck built a chapel in Saint Johnsbury, Vermont, on Dog Mountain, a four-hundred-acre farm where he and his wife live with their four dogs and a cat. The chapel Huneck built welcomes visitors and dogs from all over the world. Huneck has constructed stained glass windows celebrating dogs who graced his life, and he has placed a black Lab angel dog at the top of the chapel's steeple. At the Remembrance Wall, thousands of letters and photos from grieving people honor their dear dogs who have passed from this world.

We have had the privilege of receiving thousands of letters ourselves, from people who tell us about the animals who shared their lives. Many of their experiences deal with animals who have returned in some way to let the humans know that there is only a thin veil that separates life and death. These people know that they have experienced the soul, which once dwelled in an animal's body, communicating with them after death. Some of their stories are in this chapter.

Soon you will meet dogs who let their human companions and, in one case, a wonderful animal communicator know that dogs do, indeed, go to heaven and continue to help and protect you from the beyond.

The stories in this chapter include:

- A cocker spaniel named Freckles who keeps a military officer on the alert while guarding the president's aircraft

- Delilah, a Great Dane with a great heart, who didn't leave this earth before bringing hope to a dying cancer patient

- Sheba, a dog of divorce, who made one last visit to the man who deeply missed her

- The animal communicator and author Amelia Kinkade, who had a remarkable encounter with angel dogs who showed her what heavenly creatures dogs really are

- Tobe, a German short-haired pointer who visited the dreams of both the human and the dog he had left behind

- Typo, the rescued dog who left this earthly plane in the arms of Jesus

- And of course Taylor, who answers questions about dogs and heaven in "Ask Taylor."

We invite you to read the next stories with an open mind and a tender heart. If you let them, they will comfort you in your own experiences of loss and give you hope for being reunited with beloved dogs who have passed on.

Midnight Visit

Fred Wickert
Gilboa, New York

*D*uring my Air Force career I was stationed in Tokyo, Japan. While there, I acquired a wife, a dog, and a cat. The dog, a honey-colored cocker spaniel with a lot of white freckles on his nose, was named Freckles. We named the cat Blondie; he was yellow and white and had no tail. Fortunately, Freckles and Blondie got along with each other very well.

Freckles and I had a relationship of deep and abiding love. When the Air Force sent my wife and me back to the United States, we were not allowed to bring animals on the plane. I had to send Freckles and Blondie on a commercial flight.

I took the two animals to the airport and put them together in the same cage. They were such good friends that I knew they would be happier and less afraid on the flight if they had each other. People at the airport were amazed when they saw Freckles and Blondie snuggled in the cage side by side. Everybody knows that dogs and cats just don't mix. But these two were the best of friends.

After we picked up Freckles and Blondie upon their safe arrival at the airport in California, they traveled with my wife and me in our car all over the United States. These two animals were always with us.

Halfway through my military career, I was transferred to Andrews Air Force Base, in Maryland, to join the security forces protecting the aircraft used by the president. Freckles and Blondie went with us to this new assignment.

After five years, I went to the war in Vietnam. This time, I had to go alone and leave Freckles and my wife behind. Blondie had passed away two years earlier. When I returned home from Vietnam a little over a year later, Freckles and I were overjoyed to be together again. I had been reassigned to presidential security for the remainder of my career, so we wouldn't have to move again.

In late autumn of the following year, I got up one morning at a very early hour. Freckles woke up and joined me in the kitchen as I prepared and ate my breakfast. I petted him for a few minutes, and then he went to the coat closet inside the front door. The closet contained a folded piece of carpet on which he liked to sleep.

When I was ready to leave for work, I went to get my coat and hat from the closet. I reached down to pet Freckles and tell him good-bye. That is when I discovered that he

Fred's Freckles

had died there in the closet. I canceled my plans for the day, built him a nice casket, and gave him a decent burial.

I felt devastated by Freckles's sudden death. He had been my little buddy for so many years, and we had been through much together. I was stunned and shocked by this unanticipated loss, and I grieved for him. My wife and I had no clue that Freckles's time was nearing an end. He was old but had not been ill at all. A happy dog, he had carried out his normal routine and showed no signs of discomfort.

About a year later, I was working the midnight shift in a warm hangar, guarding the president's small airplane. There were three separate aircraft with the presidential seal on their sides parked in the same hangar. One was a Boeing 707. It was the airplane the press and public were most familiar with and usually was referred to as Air Force One. The term *Air Force One* is the code word and call sign for whichever Air Force aircraft the president is flying on. It is only Air Force One while the president is actually aboard the airplane. The smallest one in the hangar was one that most people were unaware of, a four-engine Lockheed Jet Star. This is the plane I was guarding that night. The other two planes designated for the president were a C-118 Constellation and a four-engine propeller-driven aircraft used for smaller airports where the runway wouldn't be long enough for a jet aircraft to land. One other Boeing 707 did not have the seal permanently displayed on it and was used only as a backup. Whenever the president went somewhere on the Boeing 707, the backup Boeing 707 was not far away. If for some reason there was a breakdown, they would quickly switch to the backup plane, so the president could stay on schedule. The White House fleet at the time numbered about forty aircraft.

When I worked the midnight shift that night, guarding the Lockheed Jet Star, I sat at a small table near the front of the plane. Everyone who came into this area had to sign in and out. At that hour, I was the only one there. Because of the quiet of the huge, empty aircraft hangar and the late hour, I became drowsy and, quite unintentionally, fell asleep. In the military, falling asleep on guard duty is a severely punishable offense. If you are found sleeping, you are court-martialed or severely punished. This kind of indiscretion would ruin a career and even threaten receiving a pension, no matter how long or illustrious a career you had had. Only three years remained before I would retire and be eligible to collect my pension.

Suddenly, Freckles was there on the table, licking my face. His tongue and presence woke me up. I know it wasn't a dream, because my face was wet with his saliva. I could feel him. It was real. He was there!

Just as I awoke, the security superintendent walked through the door on the other side of the hangar. He occasionally came in the middle of the night to check on the duty guard. Freckles had just saved me and my career.

Yes, Freckles had passed away more than a year before. Yet he was still with me and remained my faithful friend. Now I know that there is life after death. And I know that Freckles is my guardian angel.

Meditation

What would convince you that there is life after death? How will you know that an angel dog who has passed away is still with you?

Delilah, My Gentle Giant

Colette Muhlenkamp
Orange, California

At her birth, my precious Delilah, a Great Dane, weighed in at one pound. With that initial size, I never would have anticipated the impact such a small delight would have on my life. As she grew exponentially, it soon became clear to me that my life would never be the same now that Delilah was in it.

When she was four years old and fully grown, Delilah weighed a hefty 135 pounds. As I took her around my neighborhood, I never minded "walking the horse" — the comment that some passersby and neighbors made. Only a select few ever really knew what a gentle giant walked among us.

I was constantly amazed that children rarely showed fear when Delilah and I walked past them. As big as Delilah was, children always seemed to know that she was a friend and companion. Even children that Delilah towered over would chase after us, yelling their hellos and begging for big wet kisses from my dog. Delilah made them laugh, and their spirits lifted as they experienced her patience and unconditional friendship.

Although children never judged her, some adults quickly misjudged the big black dog. Some noticed her size and made a point of crossing the street to avoid her. How wrong they were to be intimidated by my loving dog with a generous heart big enough to match her size.

As an oncology nurse, I would trade stories about our animal friends with my patients at the hospital's outpatient cancer center. Even when patients were feeling desperately ill, they would light up and muster a smile if I shared pictures of my dog. Their favorites were photos of Delilah in the bathtub or dressed up as Rudolph the Red-Nosed Reindeer.

One patient in particular, Jolie, missed her own dog very much, since the dog was living back East with her mother and father. Jolie found joy and solace in talking about both of our dogs, but she was especially interested in Delilah. As cancer ravaged her young body, she wanted nothing more than to meet the wonderful dog whose pictures had made her smile.

On a pleasantly sunny afternoon, Delilah and I drove the twenty minutes to the hospital. With her physician's permission, Jolie came outside onto the patio in a wheelchair, pushed by her nurse, with her IV pole. We all thought a visit with Delilah would boost her spirits. I will never forget how, without my saying a word, Delilah seemed to know the purpose of this trip. Although several colleagues and family members surrounded us, Delilah darted her way through the crowd and ran directly toward the guest of honor. Even a wheelchair and IV poles could not stop the healing touch of Delilah's tongue licking Jolie's cheeks. The laughter emitted that day filled all of our hearts with the strength to keep fighting and the hope that tomorrow would be all right. Over the next couple of months, Jolie would always brighten as she fondly recalled Delilah's kisses.

One day in December 2003, I got a call from our dog walker that

Delilah was behaving oddly. I hurried home as fast as I could in the heavy rush-hour traffic. I knew the minute I opened my door and saw her that Delilah was dying. Sometimes, being a nurse is not a benefit. Delilah bled to death internally while we waited for the paramedics. Although the initial indication was ingestion of rat poison, an autopsy proved otherwise. She died of a bleeding disorder, idiopathic thrombocytopenia.

Colette and Delilah

As Delilah lay dying in my arms, she never complained, although I knew she was in excruciating pain. She laid her head in my lap and gave me a look as if to comfort me. I had been blessed with her very special companionship, and as her life slipped away, Delilah seemed to know how much I would miss her. Whether we were taking naps together, or Delilah was being my pillow or my alarm clock, I had never experienced such love as I did in the four and a half years that we were together.

I did not have the heart to tell Jolie about Delilah's passing. By moving into an office position instead of being out on the hospital floor, I made an effort to avoid Jolie, but that worked only for several weeks. When I could not delay the inevitable any longer, I had to give Jolie the sad news. She cried as if Delilah were her own. It was very humbling. Here she was, dying at twenty-seven years of age and weeping over the loss of my dog but not at her own young life fading away.

My friendship with Delilah did not end with her passing. In the several weeks that followed her death, she visited me in my dreams. In one dream, Delilah and I were at home. I was bending over to hug her, as I had always done. Everything seemed so real: the sounds of me patting her side, the breeze from her tail wagging, and the weight of her leaning in to me. It was as if she were still with me. She communicated to me that she was all right now. These dreams were so vivid that I would wake up feeling joyous, only to fall back into the reality that Delilah was gone, at least physically.

At times, my grief over Delilah's loss has been unbearable. After her passing, I was amazed at the number of people who shared my loss as if it were their own. Now I continue to find comfort in showing pictures of Delilah. I am comforted when I discover her old whiskers and hairs that should have been washed away or vacuumed up long ago. Her scent clings to her toys and blankets, and I try so desperately to preserve it. Mostly, I fear that with time these reminders will fade away. But my gentle giant continues to live in my heart and in the hearts of all who knew her. None of us will ever forget my beloved Delilah.

Meditation

Have you had dream visitations from a dog who has passed over into the invisible realms? Did these dreams comfort you with the knowledge that this dog's love continues to be a powerful blessing in your life?

Sheba's Last Visit

Howard Weiner
Springhill, Florida

efore marrying my present wife, Suzan, I was married to Terri for two years. We had a dog named Sheba whom we both loved dearly. Though she was close to both of us, Sheba seemed to bond a little closer to me.

I loved that dog and spoiled her rotten. Any extra money I had went to buy her toys and gourmet dog food. Her shiny-black, healthy coat affirmed that spoiling her was not in vain. She was full of energy, and whenever I came home, she would jump up on me and lick my face all over to show her happiness. I played with Sheba frequently, and she loved the toy ball I threw for her.

At first my marriage was a happy one, but then things started going wrong. As Terri and I began to drift apart, Sheba seemed to sense my unhappiness. She was such a wonderful dog and helped me get through the days when I felt quite saddened by the rift that was growing between Terri and me. Sheba always knew when to come over and lie on my lap to give me moral support. During that difficult time, she stayed nearby and comforted me.

At last, Terri and I decided to get a divorce. We tried a separation, but a divorce seemed inevitable. I wanted to take Sheba with me but could afford only a small studio apartment where pets were

178

not allowed. I tried to find another apartment, but to no avail. On the day I moved, I couldn't even bring myself to say good-bye to Sheba. It was too emotional for me. Tears welled up in my eyes, but I brushed them away. A grown man wasn't supposed to cry.

One night about six months later, I fell into a troubled sleep. My thoughts were of missing Sheba terribly and feeling guilty for having left her. After tossing and turning restlessly, I suddenly awoke from a dream. I opened my eyes to see Sheba's brown eyes staring into mine. I was startled and wondered how she had found her way to my studio apartment. The sight of Sheba made me happier than I had been in a long time. I reached out to stroke her and felt Sheba's soft skin. It was wonderful to be petting her once again, but in an instant she was gone. As I drifted back to sleep, I wondered why she couldn't have

Howard's Sheba

stayed with me. That night I had the first good sleep I'd experienced in months, because Sheba's presence had given me such a sense of peace and tranquillity.

The next morning, the phone rang. It was Terri. Her sobbing voice warned me that something was seriously wrong. The hair on the back of my neck stood up. She told me Sheba had suffered a heart attack and died instantly. A chill ran through me. Gathering up my courage, I asked her what time Sheba had died. Somehow, I knew Terri would say 12:30 that morning — the exact time Sheba had come to me in my apartment. I knew then that Sheba's appearance the night of her death was her way of letting me know she wasn't angry that I couldn't take her with me when I moved.

I will never forget the moment with Sheba as she left this world. It made me realize that someday I will be with my special Sheba again.

Meditation

How has a dying dog showed you that all is forgiven, but you will never be forgotten?

Our Invisible Valentines

North Hollywood, California

*L*et's say you think all this animal psychic business is a bunch of hogwash, horse-pucky, or bullfeathers. Well, you'd better hit the delete button quick, because my Valentine story is so utterly outrageous, it even popped my paradigm. Ouch. In all my years as a professional psychic, I have never witnessed anything this shocking and breathtakingly beautiful. But if you're up for a wild ride, go unplug the phone; or better yet, save it for a moment when you can kick up your feet, mix yourself a martini, and let me rocket your mind out into the galaxy at warp speed. I'm going to need your full attention.

I cried myself to sleep Christmas night and battled nightmares of convulsions for hours. The "imaginary" seizures traveled back and forth between me and my little cat, Florabelle, who slept sweetly on her pillow by my head. Of course, Ol' Flo didn't even wake up while I was being tortured. The tremors seemed to be endless. I'd pray myself back to sleep, then it would start again: shaking, shaking, and shaking.

I had no reason to be crying. Nothing terrible had happened to me. The flurry of tears and hours of night terrors had not been triggered by anything in my outer world...yet. For those of you who saw the film *Minority Report*, you know that being a "precog" is not always fun. I am like a spider on a web, connected with all creation, and when that web shakes even on the other side of the planet, I often feel the vibrations even before disaster hits.

This was my second night of emotional hell. I was gripped with terror and grief all night Christmas Eve as well. I was having a lovely holiday in my outer life, so there was no excuse for my inexplicable sadness.

Christmas Day, my mystery was solved. I don't watch television and had not yet heard about the earthquake in Iran where over twenty thousand people died and up to one hundred thousand were injured or missing. Once I got this gruesome news, I received even more sad tidings from one of my dear friends. Beth, my workshop coordinator in Memphis, emailed to say that one of her beloved dogs, Little Girl, unexpectedly died Christmas night after a series of seizures. Ahh . . . more shaking.

Little Girl was facetiously named — not unlike a two-hundred-pound python I once met named Tiny. Little Girl was a one-hundred-pound Newfoundland. She had been a friend of mine, so this was tragic news indeed. This loss caught Beth in the wake of another tremendous loss. Only a few months before, Beth's . . . resplendent Saint Bernard named Amelia Tallulah had gone on to Higher Ground. Now Beth had another agonizing loss to deal with . . . so soon.

The day after Christmas, I sat at my computer and shut my eyes. I tuned in to Little Girl to locate her whereabouts. I saw her joyously united with her best friend, Amelia Tallulah. Knowing that spirits have jobs on the Other Side, I asked Little Girl what she was doing.

"Digging," she said.

"Digging?" I asked.

"Yes," she said with urgency before she ran off to get back to work.

Then Amelia Tallulah bounded over to me, only long enough for me to give her a quick pat on her gorgeous freckled face. "I'm sorry I don't have time to talk now," she said.

"What are you doing that's so important?" I asked.

"Digging," she also said. "And I'm helping the children cross over." She hurried back to her post.

Suddenly, a bright-eyed golden retriever ran up to me, her shaggy fur as golden as the sun on a hot summer's day.

"Tell Vickie I'm here, too," the golden said. Then she ran off.

She was replaced by a rambunctious brown hound dog. "Tell Linda I said hello, and I'm here digging too!"

"Where did you know her?" I asked.

"From New Mexico. Tell her I still love her. Sorry, I gotta go," this one yelled as she raced off.

Instantly, a little black-and-white dog appeared, much smaller than all her tall, burly counterparts, but no less determined. "I'm here, too!" she said.

"Who was your mommy?" I asked.

"Connie," she said. "Tell her hello from me. Tell her that her beagle says hello." This little one, apt to get trampled underfoot, spoke with such authority, she appeared to be the commander of the troops.

"Are you sure you're a beagle?" I asked.

Take my advice, readers. I'm not using it. For every time I've instructed my students "Don't argue with the information you receive! Trust your intuition," here I was, not only arguing with a dog, I was arguing with a DEAD dog! She woofed in disgust. I waited for her to stamp her paw indignantly and yell, "What part of I'M A BEAGLE do you not understand!?" She didn't. She tried to be polite.

"Just tell Connie her beagle is here!" she said, exasperated.

I was embarrassed. "What are you doing?" I asked the little dog.

"Digging," she said.

"Where the hell am I?" I asked myself, as I looked down the row of the five angel dogs digging side by side.

I backed up to get a more panoramic view. I saw more angel dogs and more angel dogs, passionately digging. Then I saw what stood in front of this endless army of dogs. I flew above it all to get an Ariel [angel's] view.

"What the...?" I whispered.

Then...

"Oh my God!"

We were in Iran. The dogs floated in the air behind thousands of men — men who were bloody, tear-stained, and desperate, so heartbroken and exhausted they could barely stand. With shovels, picks, and their raw bare hands, they attacked mountains of rubble. Each man had an angel dog floating just off his shoulder and whispering in his ear.

"Dig!" the dogs urged. "Dig! Dig! Don't give up! Just keep digging!" Their little spirit paws whirled feverishly in the air.

I saw one man lift a child out of the rubble only to discover the child was dead. The dog near his shoulder was Little Girl. She funneled a wave of golden light into the devastated man, who heaved with sobs and almost fell to his knees as he held the child's body in his arms. Then I saw the child in spirit — upset and disoriented — until Amelia Tallulah came to her aid and ushered her safely into the Light.

I looked down the ranks at the battalion of angel dogs. All of a sudden, I saw what I had not seen before, as if yet another veil had been lifted from my sight. Tunnels of golden light joined every man with his spirit guide, as the dogs channeled energy into the men, filling them with courage, vitality, and hope.

As I flew higher to survey the terrain, I saw an army of men and troops of spirit dogs spread out in every direction endlessly. It was the most stunning vision I've ever been privy to in my life. The horror below was indescribable. The extent of the devastation, the depth of the tragedy, and the ocean of pain were equal only to the beauty of God's cavalry. Heaven had opened her doors and sent to earth her team of special forces — a battalion of weightless, timeless, tireless crusaders — all canine   but each one the very embodiment of courage and good cheer. No human angels could have handled this tragedy better.

I didn't know animals did this. I didn't know God did this. I was utterly floored.

I brought myself back to my waking world, wiped at my hot tears, and typed the dogs' messages to their former human companions. I had the strong sense that Little Girl had crossed over at that precise moment in time just to aid this cause.

Vickie Schroeder and Connie Zimet are two of my best workshop coordinators, but I had no conscious knowledge of the two dogs that came to say hello. Connie is one of my best friends, and she had never mentioned the beagle before, thus my argument with the pint-sized drill sergeant. Linda Sivertsen is one of my best friends in the world, but I knew nothing of this dog that lived with her back in New Mexico.

Vickie emailed back to say the golden retriever was Morgan Xanthe, one of her first goldens, and the dog was reddish as red could be. She had been a rescue dog, adopted from a couple who got a divorce. Vickie wrote, "Morgan Xanthe was the love of our lives. I could see where her love extends beyond all existence."

Beth emailed to say that Little Girl's passion for digging had taken its toll on her backyard for many years. And I knew that Amelia Tallulah had been a therapy dog in life, so it came as no surprise that she was helping children transition into the spirit world. When Linda called, I told her the brown hound dog looked like a cross between her two present dogs, Adobe and Digger. Linda said that Sixdance had been Adobe's sister and she did, indeed, live with her back in New Mexico. She added that Sixdance had been "quite a digger!"

But when I got Connie's email, I burst into tears. It was the biggest surprise.

Connie had spent many joyous years in love with a tough little beagle named Katie, whose air of authority dwarfed her modest height. Connie wrote to say that at first glance, she'd thought I was mistaken. She remembered Katie to be brown and white, not black and white. But when she rooted out pictures of Katie, she saw that the little Snoopy-model was indeed more black than brown. I called Connie, laughing and crying, and Connie said, "Yes, that Katie was quite a digger!"

Animals are not what they seem. Our world is not what it seems. With the Descartes-dominated notions of the prior century gradually falling away, we are able to prove that animals can think and feel. I challenge you to expand your awareness even further. The galaxy that God has created is not random. It is not the cruel, mechanical gearbox medieval scientists led us to believe. There is comfort, order, and Grace in the universe. Animals are more magical than any of us could ever dream. So is your world . . . and so are you!

This love letter is devoted to your Invisible Valentines. No one knows where Sonata in C was before Mozart composed it, or where David was hiding before Michelangelo freed him from a slab of marble. Where was Middle Earth before Tolkien brought it down from heaven? Do artists work alone? Or are they surrounded by invisible cherubs who might be sporting more than wings? Perhaps their muses have whiskers or hooves or fluffy tails or sharp claws with tufts of fur between their toes. Do any of us work alone?

Maybe, just maybe, you've got an angel on your shoulder, too, giving you the impetus to write, to paint, to sing, to dance, to design one more website, to see one more patient, to heal an aching relationship, or even just to help you "dig" through the paperwork on your desk. Close your eyes and say "hello" to someone who still loves you, a spirit sweetheart who may have left her body on earth but not her soul.

Here's to you, Little Girl, Amelia T, Morgan, Sixdance, and Katie, and to all my readers' angel dogs who, unbeknownst to you, saved lives in Iran. And here's to my Archangel, the source of my inspiration.

Mr. Jones, no matter where you are in heaven or on earth, you are the sunlight in my universe.

Meditation

Who are the angels on your shoulders, helping you dig through your tragedies and painful experiences or inspiring you to create a better life for yourself?

My Dog and I Shared a Dream

Julie Olson
San Rafael, California

Tobe, our dear baby boy German short-haired pointer, died of cancer. A seizure caused him to go into a coma. We knew we had to let him go back home to God. We feel grateful to have had this compassionate, humorous, gentle, and loving soul in our family for seven years, but the pain of his leaving was almost too much for us to bear at first. Shanti and Tuza, our two girl dogs who were also of the same breed, missed Tobe too.

During the long, sad drive home from the vet's office, where we said our tearful good-byes to Tobe, I closed my eyes and rested. Immediately I saw Tobe in my mind's eye, on a patio with a shallow reflecting pool in front of him. He was covered with a blanket and lying on one also. He looked peaceful, relaxed, and rather pleased with himself. A being who wore long, ancient-Greek-type garments stood nearby, attending to Tobe. I instinctively knew that this being loved Tobe even more than I did. Until that moment, I would have thought this to be an impossibility, because I loved Tobe so much. The sense that Tobe was well cared for by the spiritual guardian eased my grief. As part of this inner-world scene, I saw five yellow butterflies dancing above Tobe's head. Other animals, who seemed to know Tobe and love him, were also around. Almost as quickly as the vision had started, the scene faded. I opened my eyes and told my husband, Paul, what I'd experienced.

A few weeks later, on a cold day, Paul and I walked along a favorite trail with Shanti and Tuza. We talked about how much we loved and missed Tobe. We laughed about some of Tobe's antics: the way he would run into a room and make a wide sweep, grabbing anything in his mouth that wasn't tied down as an invitation for us to chase him. Or the way he batted the paper out of our hands if we blocked our view of him standing at our feet waiting for affection. His paw would hit us on the knee and stay there,

Julie and Paul's Tuza, Shanti, and Tobe

with Tobe looking expectant until we gave him some love. Just as we were reminiscing, a yellow butterfly, similar to the ones I had seen in my vision after Tobe's passing, danced across the path in front of us. Paul and I knew that seeing this butterfly in the winter was a heaven-sent kiss from Tobe.

After Tobe died, we moved our other two dogs into our bedroom, so they could sleep next to us. One night, I had a dream that all three of the dogs and I were in a large park with huge old-growth oak trees and soft rolling hills. Tuza was off by herself, sniffing the ground near a pile of rustling dry leaves. Over a little rise I could see Tobe with Shanti. In this dream I was carrying a little device in my hand that showed me where the three dogs were at all times.

As the dream continued, Tobe and Shanti played together. They had always been good buddies while Tobe was alive. Suddenly the two dogs ran toward me, with Tobe playfully chasing Shanti down the hill to where I stood. They both looked happy and free.

At that moment in my dream, 2:45 A.M., I awoke abruptly and so did my husband. We looked over to where Shanti lay sleeping in her bed. She was making the most unusual barking noise that we'd ever heard. Her eyes were closed but moving, as they do when she's dreaming. Her barking had been loud enough to wake us out of a sound sleep at exactly the instant in my dream when Shanti was running with Tobe down the hill toward me.

I know it has been reported that people sometimes dream the same thing at the same time. But that night, I had the distinct impression that Shanti and I had been sharing our dream. This dream of Tobe in heaven was so vivid that we both experienced it as reality.

I think of the dream with Tobe that Shanti and I shared as a gift from God. Through it, I was able to be with my precious Tobe once again. I felt the continuation of all the love Tobe gave to us, and the love that our family of dogs and humans had given to him.

Meditation

Have you watched your dog dreaming? Have you wondered about the reality of dreams? Could a dog show you that the dream world is a doorway to heaven?

Typo, the Dog Who Was No Mistake

Sarah Casey Newman
St. Louis, Missouri

*T*ypo was the baby I never had. She entered my life as a stray when she was still a puppy and I was grieving over the loss of Oliver, the first dog I'd ever had as an adult. Oliver, another angel dog, spent only the last three of his twelve years with me. He had arrived unexpectedly and anchored me during one of life's major emotional storms. When the storm finally passed, Oliver left almost as suddenly as he had come, leaving a hole in my heart that I was sure no other dog could fill.

A few months after Oliver's death, while volunteering at a local animal shelter, I was drawn to a little stray dog with mesmerizing eyes. It was love at first sight, but I hated the thought of replacing Oliver. (As if any angel animal we've loved and lost could ever be replaced.) Knowing I should seek permission from the rest of my family before even thinking about adopting the cute little creature, I headed for home.

My husband, Buck, and stepdaughter, Shannon, returned to the shelter with me the next day. It was nearly closing time. With thoughts of missing Oliver still on my mind, I was half-hoping the little pup had been adopted, but such was not the case. There she was in her kennel, looking as if she'd been waiting for us.

We took her to a playroom and plopped her on the floor. She scurried straight to me. I aimed her at my husband; she scurried back to me. I directed her toward Shannon; back she came. Still, I refused to give in to her charms. I wasn't sure I was ready for another dog, because the pain of losing Oliver lingered. Also, I felt as if I were being disloyal to Oliver by giving my heart to another dog so soon. It didn't occur to me that Oliver might be orchestrating a meeting of hearts between me and this dog who was in need of a home.

We returned the little temptress to her kennel and stepped outside to debate the issue. When Buck and Shannon outvoted my weak objections, we went back inside to adopt the scraggly cutie just as another couple was arriving at a similar decision. Had we waited only a moment longer, the much-debated dog would have gone home with them. I knew then that this little dog was meant to be part of my life.

Sarah's Typo

We named her Typo because she seemed like a mistake, a mixture of...what? Yorkie, poodle, Lhasa, shih tzu...take your pick. She had long, flowing, off-white fur, over-sized ears that looked suspiciously like wings, and the most angelic little dog-face I'd ever seen. For the next fourteen years, Typo was either at my feet, on my lap, or by my side. In my eyes she was always perfect, although she developed a heart murmur and liver problems later in life. When Typo was twelve, her health started to fail noticeably. Sometimes she would fall over and have trouble breathing but would recover; my heart almost stopped when I watched her in such distress.

Then my mother became ill, and I, an only child, packed up Typo and drove seven hundred miles to Pennsylvania to care for her. We stayed at my mother's house for nine months. During that time, and for nearly a year after my mother's death, Typo's symptoms virtually vanished. Her poor health ceased being a constant cause of worry and concern, and instead Typo became a steady source of comfort and strength for me.

Only after our lives returned to normal did Typo's health begin to fail once more, this time rapidly. For the first time in my life, I was forced to make the most heart-wrenching decision that anyone who has loved and been loved by one of God's furry angels can make. Typo's veterinarians explained to me what her body was doing, how painful for her it could be at the end of her life, and how short our remaining time together would be. But it was Typo who told me when it was time to say good-bye. I only had to look into her eyes to see that there was no longer any joy in them, only a sad, silent plea for me to release her. I knew I had to make that fatal call.

On the evening that I made the final decision to let go of Typo, the vet agreed to come to the house. It was the middle of June. Shannon was away at summer school, and my husband was gone on a business trip. Like so many of our previous travels, this was a journey Typo and I would take only with each other.

I lit the way with a roomful of candles. I put on the softest, most heavenly sounding music I could find. I spent the rest of the afternoon holding my beloved companion, talking to and praying over her. I read stories to her about the place between heaven and earth where our beloved animal companions look forward to having our companionship once again, the Rainbow Bridge. I read *All God's Creatures Go to Heaven*, a children's book by Amy Nolfo-Wheeler with wonderful paintings by Nancy Noel, about the child angels who love and care for our animals while they wait for us in heaven. I tried to comfort myself as much as I hoped I was comforting Typo with promises that we would be together again someday.

Determined to be strong for her sake, to not let her see the pain I was feeling, I cradled Typo in my arms as the vet injected the fatal fluid. I hugged and stroked her and whispered words of love and gratitude into her fur until her breathing stopped and she was still. I stayed strong even as the vet carried Typo's lifeless little body out the door of my home. And then the pain hit with a vengeance. I plunged so quickly and deeply into despair that I collapsed on the floor in hysterical tears. Sobbing uncontrollably for what felt like forever, I finally screamed out to God, "I need help and I need it NOW!"

In a moment, the tears were gone, and Typo was there. The vision of her was so real and clear to me that I felt I could reach out and touch her. Equally as real was the bearded man in a blazing-white robe who held Typo in his arms as she wagged her tail ecstatically and covered his face with kisses. I had no doubt that the man I saw in my vision was Jesus. When he put his arm around me, I felt the greatest peace I have ever known. Also, I experienced the greatest joy I had ever felt, knowing then that Typo had not died. She had simply returned home. She was happier than I could ever have imagined. And now she was sharing her happiness with me.

Hardly aware of how I got there, I found myself on my feet, dancing and laughing, praising God as uncontrollably as I had sobbed only moments before. I couldn't help myself. I overflowed with joy, while a smile spread across my face and my heart.

Six years later, memories of Typo and of that mystical moment after her death continue to comfort me. The smile in my heart has never left. And I know, as surely as I know how dearly I loved her, that Typo, my four-footed angel with fur, is still with me.

Meditation

If you closed your eyes now and remembered the moment of a beloved dog's death, could you visualize Jesus, a guardian angel, or a spiritual teacher embracing and welcoming the newest dog to the Rainbow Bridge?

Ask Taylor

Dear Taylor,

Do dogs go to heaven? Will we meet our animal companions again and be reunited with them? Do our dog friends remember us?

Sincerely,
Ever So Hopeful

Dear Hopeful,

Yes, yes, and yes some more. Dogs definitely go to heaven. Would it really be heaven without them? Our love and our spirits never die, even though our bodies may be gone. We are as faithful to you in the afterlife as we were when we walked beside you on earth. Sit very still, close your eyes, and feel the

touch of our heavenly kisses upon your cheek. We
will never leave you.

Faithfully yours,

Taylor

When our dear golden retriever Prana died, we cried for days.
We missed her passionately. It felt as if all the light, all the color had
drained out of our world. But we were blessed with dreams of her.
There was a sacred temple grounds on which she used to love to run
and to explore while she was alive. In these dreams after Prana's

death, we saw her as the guardian
dog of a spiritual temple in the
inner heavens. She would come to
us in the dream state, wag her tail,
and run off to do whatever her new
duties are at this inner-world temple.
Her body looked healthy; it was no
longer ravaged by cancer or causing
her to suffer. She was letting us
know that her life had gone on, and
ours should too.

Almost two years after Prana
died, she came to Allen in a dream,
out of an ocean, carrying a tiny
puppy in her mouth. She deposited

Allen and Linda's Prana

the puppy at Allen's feet and looked at him as if to say: Here's your
new playmate. This dream occurred on the night before we went to

a farm to visit a litter of yellow Labs. When Allen saw the pup who would become our sweet little companion Taylor, he recognized her from the dream. She must have known him too, or at least Prana had taught her how to choose us. Just as Prana had done, when we had met her years before in a litter of puppies, now Taylor came over and untied Allen's shoelace. He picked Taylor up, embraced her, and she was ours from that moment on, at least physically. Spiritually, she had been brought to us by a divine messenger in Allen's dream of the night before, emerging from an ocean of love.

We hope you have enjoyed reflecting upon your experiences with the Angel Dogs who bring light into your life. As we wrote this book, we felt Angel Dogs nearby, helping us to choose the words and images that would tell you of their love, the stories that would let you know they have been and will forever be your friends.

Notes

Introduction

Epigraph: Caroline Knapp, *Pack of Two: The Intricate Bond between People and Dogs* (New York: The Dial Press, 1998), p. 20.

1   Stanley Coren, *How Dogs Think: Understanding the Canine Mind* (New York: Free Press, 2004), pp. 5–6.

2   Jennifer Leonard, quoted in Michael D. Lemonick, "The Mother of All Dogs," *Time*, December 2, 2002, pp. 78–80.

3   Peter Savolainen, quoted in Ibid.

4   AustralianMedia.com, "History of Dogs" (Australian Media Pty Ltd., 2001–2005), http://www.dogquotes.com/historyofdogs.htm.

5   Brad Zellar, "Man's Best Friend — and Much, Much More," review of

A Dog's History of America, by Mark Derr, *Minneapolis Star Tribune,* September 24, 2004.

6   PetPlace Veterinarians, "The History of Dogs and Native Americans" (PetPlace.com 1999–2005), http://www.petplace.com/Articles/ artShow.asp?artID=1221.

7   "How Dog Came to the Indians — an Ojibwe Story," http://www.samoyed.org/dogind.html.

8   Brother Christopher, quoted in Mary Ann Sullivan, "Dogs: How They Teach Families about Love," *National Catholic Register,* June 22–28, 2003, p. 15.

9   Joseph Wood Krutch, *The Best of Two Worlds* (New York: William Sloane Associates, 1950), quoted in Jeffrey Moussaieff Masson and Susan McCarthy, *When Elephants Weep: The Emotional Lives of Animals* (New York: Delacorte Press, 1995), p. 223.

10 American Pet Products Manufacturers Association, 2003–2004 National Pet Owners Survey, posted November 11, 2003, on www.appma.org.

11 "Shopping Hounds: Retailers Go to the Dogs by Inviting Them In," *USA Weekend,* July 9–11, 2004.

Chapter One: Have You Received Loyalty and Friendship from Divine Messenger Dogs?

Epigraph: Kristin von Kreisler, *The Compassion of Animals: True Stories of Animal Courage and Kindness* (Rocklin, Calif.: Prima Publishing, 1997), p. 257.

1   Ahmed Tharwat, "Fear of Terrorism Yields to Love for Puppies," *Minneapolis Star Tribune,* February 23, 2003, quoted with permission of the author, www.belahdan.com.

2   Study by Karen Allen discussed in John O'Neil, "Behavior: A Best Friend in Times of Stress," *New York Times,* October 1, 2002, http://www.nytimes.com/2002/10/01/health/psychology/ 1034567296&ei=1&en=cf1da29f27b1af36.

3   National Pet Owner Survey, American Animal Hospital Association, http://www.aahanet.org/.

4   Catherine Mills and John C. Wright, quoted in Janet McConnaughey, "Baby Swings Might Trigger Dog Attacks, Coroner Says," *Minneapolis Star Tribune*, February 24, 2005.

Chapter Two: What If Heroes Have Four Paws and Fur?

Epigraph: Excerpted from *Animals Are Soul Too!* by Harold Klemp, 2005 Eckankar. Used by permission of Eckankar, P.O. Box 2000, Chanhassen, Minnesota 55317, www.eckankar.org. All rights reserved.

1   Rupert Sheldrake, *Dogs That Know When Their Owners Are Coming Home: And Other Unexplained Powers of Animals* (New York: Crown Publishers, 1999), p. 245.

Chapter Three: Can You Catch Joyrides on Wagging Tails?

Epigraph: Robert Frost, "Canis Major," *Complete Poems of Robert Frost* (New York: Holt, Rinehart, and Winston, 1964), p. 331.

Chapter Four: Are Dogs Your Divine Prescription
for Better Health?

Epigraph: Dr. Marty Becker with Danelle Morton, *The Healing Power of Pets: Harnessing the Amazing Ability of Pets to Make and Keep People Happy and Healthy* (New York: Hyperion, 2002), p. 185.

1   Dr. Marty Becker, quoted in S. W., "Heal Boy! Your Furry Companion May Be a Doctor in Disguise," *My Generation,* November–December 2002, p. 20.

2   Dr. John Church, quoted in Eileen Dent, "Cancer Diagnosis Gone to the Dogs: Clever Canines Detect Bladder Cancer from Urine Samples," *National Review of Medicine*, October 15, 2004, vol. 1, no. 19, www.nationalreviewofmedicine.com/issue/2004/10_15/clinical10_19.html.

3   Edward Creagen, MD, quoted in Arden Moore, "Get a Pet — Doctor's

Orders! Man's Best Friend May Be Your Best Medicine," *Prevention*, November 2002, pp. 177–80.

4   "Rx for a Better Life? Get a Pet, and Do It Now," *Science Daily*, November 5, 2001, http://www.sciencedaily.com/releases/ 2001/11/011105073501.htm.

5   Linda Hogan, "First People," in *Intimate Nature: The Bond between Women and Animals*, ed. Linda Hogan, Deena Metzger, and Brenda Peterson (New York: Fawcett Books, 1998), p. 12.

Chapter Five: Have Dogs Discovered the Doorways to Heaven?

Epigraph: J. Allen Boone, *Kinship with All Life: Simple, Challenging, Real-Life Experiences Showing How Animals Communicate with Each Other and with People Who Understand Them* (New York: HarperSanFrancisco, 1954), p. 64.

1   "The New Animal Spirituality: Do All Dogs Go to Heaven?" http://www.religionwriters.com/public/tips/090303/090303b.shtml.

Contributors
and Photographers

Foreword

WILLARD SCOTT appears regularly on NBC's *The Today Show* and is the author of *If I Knew It Was Going to Be This Much Fun, I Would Have Become a Grandparent First* and *The Older the Fiddle, the Better the Tune: The Joys of Reaching a Certain Age*.

Chapter One: Have You Received Loyalty and Friendship from Divine Messenger Dogs?

CHARLES PATRICK DUGAN, "Cpl. J. R. Dugan Honors a Fallen Soldier." Charles Patrick Dugan is retired from law enforcement, the

Marine Corps, and from being a college instructor. He is a Vietnam combat veteran. In Vietnam he served as a United States Marine Corps machine gunner 0331/recon marine. His BS is from Stephen F. Austin State University and his MEd is from Sul Ross State University.

DIANA JOHNSON, "An Angel in the Night," as told to Mary J. Yerkes. Diana lives in Plano, Texas, with her husband, Forrest, their five children — eight-year-old twins, Brianna and Forrest, seven-year-old Taylor, and four-year-old twins, Branden and Lauren. Zeke is a major part of the family. Diana is also a Girl Scout leader who enjoys camping and outdoor activities.

MARY J. YERKES, "An Angel in the Night." Mary is a freelance writer from Virginia. Her work appears in magazines, e-zines, anthologies, and devotional guides. To learn more, visit www.maryyerkes.com.

JAY WILLIAMS, "Lee County Prisoners Give Life to Death Row Dogs." Jay loves dogs, cars, pizzas, and NASCAR. Jay grew up with dogs and became one of the best trainers in the Lee County Sheriff's Department Cell Dogs Program. After serving his term, Jay plans to go back to school.

FRANK and LEIGH ANN GIBSON, "Postscript from Cell Dog Hershey." Frank and Leigh Ann live in Florida with their two sons, Dustin and Dylan, and their cell dog, Hershey.

JILL KELLY, "A Puppy's Love Prepared Me for Motherhood." Jill and her husband, Greg, live in their dream house in Alpharetta, Georgia, with their son, Jack, and two boxer dogs, Emeril and Elle'. Jill is a radio news broadcaster on *KICKS 101.5 Morning Show* in Atlanta. She has a happy, smiling face even after having to keep the guys in line all morning. Before working in Atlanta she worked in the Augusta, Oklahoma City, Tulsa, and Columbia, South Carolina, radio markets. Jill is a 1986 graduate of Oklahoma State University.

WAYNE AERNI, "Temujin's Spiritual Message." Wayne lives on the edge of open desert in Sun Lakes, Arizona. He and his wife, Gloria, share their life with one dog and two cats. He continually takes long quiet walks in the desert.

PAT EISENBERGER, "Casey: A Warrior of the Heart Brings Love to a Nursing Home." Pat lives in Michigan with her husband, Dale, and their shelties Casey and Cory. She is a secretary who plays the harp and quilts.

BILL MANN, "They're Still Walking." Bill is a singer-songwriter living near Nashville, Tennessee. He can be contacted by email at yourheartknows@comcast.net and at http://www.wearesoul.com.

Chapter Two: What If Heroes Have Four Paws and Fur?

CAROLINE KANE AQUIAR, "Tequila, the Matchmaker Dog Who Saved a Family." Caroline lives with her husband, Raul, and two teenage children, Ricky and Christine. Caroline is pursuing her love of writing while she and her husband work as owners/operators of their guest ranch in Ensenada, Baja, Mexico. Although Tequila died ten years ago, when their guests ask Raul and Caroline how they met, time and time again, they tell the story of Tequila, the dog who helped create and save a family. Caroline can be reached by email at rcaquiar@telnor.net.

DEL LANGHELD, "Poni Faces a Poisonous Rattlesnake." Del is a forty-seven-year-old mother of one son, Chris Herrington. In 1998, she met her soul mate, Tommy Langheld. They were married on September 3, 1999. Del works for the Webster Parish Library in Minden, Louisiana, and Tommy works as a truck driver. Their home is filled with much love for ten beautiful cats and one wonderfully courageous dog, Poni.

JEANNE CROUD, "The Puppy Who Belonged to No One." Jeanne enjoys doing beadwork and genealogy. She and her family live in Minnesota. Her daughter, Anj, has grown up to be a lovely young woman. Anj continues to have an uncanny connection with animals and plans a career in equine management.

PAM THORSEN, "Gracie, Our Hostess Dog." Pam owns Thorwood and Rosewood Inns in historic Hastings, Minnesota, with her husband, Dick. She is working on a memoir of restorations and recipes. You can reach her at www.thorwoodinn.com.

RICHARD and MARJORIE DOUSE, "Bonnie, Our Everyday Hero." Richard and Marjorie live in St. Paul, Minnesota. Before retirement, Richard was a Presbyterian minister, and Marjorie was the church organist and music director.

Chapter Three: Can You Catch Joyrides on Wagging Tails?

BOB SHAW, "Pinkey." Bob is an award-winning writer with his work published on the Internet and in newspaper columns. He has co-authored four books in the United States and the Netherlands.

KATHY BRODERICK, "Incident at Lake Isabella." Kathy is a writer living with her family in Chicago, where they are anticipating the arrival of a new schnauzer puppy.

PAMELA JENKINS, "The Booger Dog." Pamela is the office manager of her husband's veterinary clinic. She enjoys writing about the loving bond between people and their pets.

LYNDRA HEARN ANTONSON, "A Tender Solution for a Tough Problem." Lyndra empowers people to manifest their dreams and live with joy through life coaching by phone. After a lifetime of searching, she recently found and married her true love, Dale. They live happily outside Minneapolis with their animal children, Presty the dog and Binx the cat. She can be reached at lyndra@earthlink.net.

MONIQUE MUHLENKAMP, "Sierra, the Dog Who Taught Me to Live in the Moment." Monique is an award-winning photographer, writer, and publicist. She is currently the manager of the publicity department at New World Library. She lives with her husband, Steve, in an 1850s cottage in Northern California.

ELEANOR GARRELL BERGER, "Leading the Way." Eleanor writes personal commentaries for regional public radio. She has written for breed publications and was a columnist for *Good Dog! Magazine*.

ROBERTA BEACH JACOBSON, "Dog Day." Roberta is an American writer who makes her home on a remote Greek island. She is a member of the Cat Writers' Association, and her work has appeared in twenty-two anthologies. http://www.travelwriters.com/Roberta.

Chapter Four: Are Dogs Your Divine Prescription for Better Health?

ASHLEY PHELPS, "Haley, the Angel Dog Who Helped Me through Cancer." Ashley lives in Oregon with her parents, brother, and sister. She was diagnosed with Hodgkin's lymphoma on February 11,

2004, and is now in remission and a proud cancer survivor. Ashley is writing her first book.

SHAREN MEYERS, "More about Haley." Sharen Meyers is a social worker in the Pacific Northwest with experience in a mental health setting, cancer treatment, and hospice work. She now has a golden retriever puppy named Taylor whom she is raising and training to be a therapy-work partner.

SALLY ROSENTHAL, "Angel in Waiting." Sally Rosenthal and Boise are Pals for Life volunteers and live in Philadelphia with Sally's husband and cats. Sally is a contributing author to animal magazines and anthologies.

MARION T. COCHRANE, "How a Freezing Dog Warmed Our Hearts." Marion is a guardian for the ASPCA of New York, a supporter of a number of shelters in her area, and an advocate for the wild kingdom at-large. Golden retrievers Bail and Sedona, felines Sami and Olivia, and CoCo, her cockatiel, reside with Marion in their home in Northport, New York.

PATTI COLE, "Joshua B. Dawg's Lamp of Faith." Patti is a strong animal-welfare advocate. She resides in North Carolina and is the best mom a dog could ever have. "Lamp of Faith" is based on an article of the author's that appeared in the summer 2001 issue of *laJoie*, a Batesville, Virginia–based publication dedicated to the reverence for all life.

BINA AITCHISON ROBINSON, "Shep's Connection with Andy." Bina and her husband, Dave, established the Swain Ski Slopes in 1948. Bina lives on her 750-acre animal reserve, which she still patrols even as an octogenarian. She has been an animal rights and welfare activist for over thirty years, is a vegan, a prolific writer, and has published several animal-oriented newsletters. She authors an antivivisection website, www.linkny.com/~civitas/. She and Dave have four children and seven grandchildren.

A. M. ROBINSON, "Shep's Connection with Andy." Andy (A. M. Robinson) lives in Swain, New York, with his wife, Sonja, and nine-year-old twin sons, David and Colin, cat Snickers, and dog Shep, named in honor of his previous dog Shep. Andy is a local businessman who owns and operates Downhill Drew's restaurant in Swain. Swain receives more than a hundred inches of snow per year, and Andy plows the driveways of everyone in town.

DEBORAH STRAW, "Wanda, My Angel and Therapist." Deborah is a freelance writer and teacher from Vermont. Her book *Why Is Cancer Killing Our Pets* has been reissued under the title *The Healthy Pet Manual: A Guide to the Prevention and Treatment of Cancer.*

Chapter Five: Have Dogs Discovered the Doorways to Heaven?

FRED WICKERT, "Midnight Visit." Fred lives with his wife, birds, and animals in Gilboa, New York, in the Catskill Mountains. He takes care of developmentally disabled people in their homes.

COLETTE MUHLENKAMP, "Delilah, My Gentle Giant." Colette is a certified oncology registered nurse and has been in practice for eight years. In her spare time she is learning to garden and enjoys watching movies and taking pictures. She has a twelve-year-old cat named Daisy and is hoping to be blessed with another dog soon.

209

HOWARD WEINER, "Sheba's Last Visit." Howard is a writer with his poems and fillers published in *Mature Living, The Saturday Evening Post,* and *Poetry Press.*

AMELIA KINKADE, "Our Invisible Valentines." Reprinted with permission from "Amelia's Wild-Life Newsletter," February 2004. Amelia is the author of *Straight from the Horse's Mouth: How to Talk to Animals and Get Answers* and the upcoming *The Language of Miracles* (New World Library). She is a celebrated international speaker who teaches workshops and assists animals in sanctuaries all over the world. She can be reached through www.ameliakinkade.com.

JULIE OLSON, "My Dog and I Shared a Dream." Julie is a visual artist and she teaches art at the Academy of Art University in San Francisco. She was the illustrator for *Make the Connection* by Bob Greene and Oprah Winfrey and *Angel Animals: Exploring Our Spiritual Connection with Animals* by Allen and Linda Anderson. She lives with her husband, Paul, and her dogs, Kojo and Bika, in San Rafael, California.

SARAH CASEY NEWMAN, "Typo, the Dog Who Was No Mistake." Sarah is the pet writer for the *St. Louis Post-Dispatch* and personal servant for three rescued greyhounds, one rescued puppy mill dog (half-pug, half–Brussels griffon), and four cats.

Additional Photographers

Except for the following, the photographs accompanying each story in this book were taken by the contributing authors or Allen and Linda Anderson.

page 12   Photograph by Teresa Madak, Marietta, Georgia

page 35   Photograph by Stan Nelson, Bokeelia, Florida

page 93   Photograph by Ron Ward, Raleigh, North Carolina

page 116   Photograph by Robin J. Brown, Plattsburgh, New York

page 117   Photograph by Michael G. DiNunzio, Plattsburgh, New York

page 134   Photograph by Sharen Meyers, Bend, Oregon

page 141   Photograph by Stefanie Johnson, DeKalb, Illinois

Acknowledgments

*W*e give our sincere appreciation to Georgia Hughes, New World Library's editorial director, who helped us in our quest to share these amazing stories about the spiritual connection between people and dogs. Georgia, your love and encouragement have been our beacon.

We are grateful to copy editor Jacqueline Volin, typesetter Tona Pearce Myers, cover designer Bill Mifsud, our enthusiastic publicist Monique Muhlenkamp, the wise marketing director and associate publisher Munro Magruder, the wonderful visionary Marc Allen, and to all the staff at New World Library.

A hearty and sincere thank-you to Harold Klemp and to Joan Klemp for inspiring us on our journey of giving service by writing books about the animal-human spiritual bond, and for a fantastic new animal book of their own.

We want to thank our Angel Dogs Story Contest judges: Christine Davis, R. Dale Hylton, and Marcia Pruett Wilson. We also want to thank Lee County Sheriff's Captain Tom Weaver for his tireless help in our search for that special cell dogs story that would demonstrate how much good the Lee County Cell Dogs Program is doing for inmates and the dogs they train.

Love and gratitude to all those who have contributed their stories to *Angel Dogs*. Your generosity and goodwill made this book possible. Our special appreciation to the people who have endorsed the book.

We also extend our heartfelt gratitude to Stephanie Kip Rostan of Levine-Greenberg Literary Agency, Inc., our dynamo literary agent with the heart of a poet.

For help in letting people know about Angel Animals in print and on the radio and television, we thank Shirley MacLaine, Willard Scott, Lessandra MacHamer, Jill Kelly, Sarah Casey Newman, Brad Woodard, Pat Miles, Alicyn Leigh, Sally Rosenthal, Deborah Bodine, Gary and Insiah Beckman, Echo Bodine, Tim Miejan, Teri Kelsh, Hal Abrams, Cynthia Brian, John Sebastian, Donna Seebo, Patricia Raskin, and the wonderfully compassionate Jonathan W. Greenfield, DVM, with his *The Family Pet* show on Long Island, New York.

We are grateful to the many bookstores that invited contributing authors to do signings and events. For our own bookstore events, we are especially grateful to Jo Gilbertson, who graciously hosts the launch of our books at the Barnes & Noble in Eden Prairie, Minnesota; Shelly Grokowski, regional director of marketing for Borders; Wendy Thorson and Paul Bartlett at Borders in Richfield, Minnesota; Terry Kraus, manager of Borders/Library Ltd. in St. Louis; Holly Stein, who has been promoted to the Borders marketing department in Ann Arbor, Michigan; Gayle Seminara-Mandel at Transitions Bookplace in Chicago; and Betty Redmond of Publishers Group West, who always makes certain we have a great time at UMBA. We appreciate the support of Rose Ryan, associate librarian at St. Louis Park Community Library. And special thanks to Patricia Gift, former editor of One Spirit Book Club, for selecting our books and giving them such a boost in the catalogs.

Sheila Bontreger, who has been our dear friend for many years and a wonderful pet sitter, has enabled us to meet readers (and animals) all over the country.

We appreciate the encouragement and support of Barbara Buckner, Arlene and Aubrey Forbes, Josse Ford, Daniel Tardent, Gail Roeske, Joyce Hofer, Margo Hendricks, Sharon and Ron Ward, Diane Burkitt, Carol Frysinger, Bettine Clemen, Kristy Walker, Catherine Gray, Barbara Morningstar, Diana and Henry Stewart-Koster, Doug and April Munson, Mary Carroll Moore, Caroline Veno, Barbara J. Gislason, and Amelia Kinkade.

Our families instilled a love of dogs and all animals in us from an early age. We feel a special appreciation to Allen's mother, Bobbie Anderson, and Linda's mother and father, Darrell and Gertrude Jackson, and Linda's sister and brother-in-law, Janet and Mario Chavez.

To our son and daughter, Mun Anderson and Susan Anderson, you're the best. We hope this book brings back fond memories of Prana.

Special thank-you to Darby Davis, editor of *Awareness*, for publishing "Pet Corner" for so many years, and Kathy DeSantis, for her beautiful book reviews.

We have sincere appreciation for those who support us as writers: The Loft Literary Center and Mary Cummings; the Minnesota Screenwriters Workshop, especially Chris Velasco; the ECK Writer's Group; and the Thursday Night Writers.

Over the years, thousands of people from all over the globe have shared their amazing dog stories with us. Thank you to the Angel Animals Network visitors and *Angel Animals Story of the Week* readers for their letters and stories.

And thanks to our animal editors: Taylor, Speedy, Cuddles, and Sunshine. Without you, we wouldn't know what animals think.